TURN THE PAGE TODAY

Mark Brown

TURN THE PAGE TODAY

Copyright © 2015 by Mark Brown

Published by The Voice Publishing

ISBN-13:978-1508619253

ISBN-10:1508619255

All scripture references, unless otherwise indicated, are taken from the Holy Bible, New Living Translation and King James Version.

Strong's Concordance King James Bible by Dr. James Strong printed originally 1890

This book is dedicated to my wife Veronica Escobedo Brown and my two sons Mark II and Matthew. You are the apple of my eye. You are the greatest gifts God could have given me. I feel honored to call Veronica my wife for life and honored to be Dad to my boys. I love you.

ACKNOWLEDGEMENTS

To my wife and sons, I love you with all my heart. God gave me a gift when He gave me each of you. Thank you for releasing me to fulfill my call, standing with me and by me through every season. You are all my treasure.

To Bishop Holcomb and Pastor Val, your profound teaching of the word helped shape who I am today. You opened your platform to me, you have spent countless hours pouring into me and I am honored to be part of your legacy. I am proud to carry the baton to reach the next generation. Thank you for your love and continued support.

To my mother in law Gracie Escobedo, you have loved me as you own son, thank you. To my in laws, Victor and Melissa Hernandez, Vanessa Weis and Adan Escobedo III, you have always believed in my dreams, supported the call and the vision as if it were your own. My heart thanks you all for your unrelenting support.

To my parents Rev. Danny and Jill Brown, thank you for providing a godly foundation and for the prayers that have covered me over time. I am proud to carry on our family legacy and come from a lineage of ministers. To my brother Jacob, you are my best friend and I can always count on you. To my sisters Angela and Jessica, thank you for your love and support.

To the late Rev. Crawford: I was 22 years old when you told me to write a book. You encouraged me to release the dream inside. You saw what God called me to be when others put it down. You taught me to focus on the vision God placed in my heart. Thank you for your encouragement.

I would like to appreciate and acknowledge the various contributions and support received for this project. Growing up in a ministerial family, I heard countless sermons; stories and presentations shared through family, friends, members of the congregation and various people I have met around the country. I believe in giving honor to whom honor is due and although I may not remember the exact source of a story I would like to thank all those who have touched my life with their life's journey. In a few cases we have changed the names to protect the privacy of individuals as I pass on their story as a blessing

to others; for the glory of God.

TABLE OF CONTENTS

INTRODUCTION

This book is for every person who has forged forward through life's difficulties, traumas, and dilemmas. If you have ever felt short changed, held onto broken pieces of the past or felt as though it was impossible to move on, yet, day after day, it seemed you just existed as life passed by; today is your day to turn the page. I know the pain of your experience was real. It hurt and it's hard to understand why it happened. I want you to know that your experience will not be wasted. God will use the amalgamation of your life experiences to produce a masterpiece. You were born for greatness. You were created and destined to be and do more than what you are doing today. As you read this book, get ready for destiny and purpose to collide. The promise and purpose that was predestined for your life when you were born will come to pass. All of the no's you have heard in life do not outweigh the yes's preordained for your future. God has scheduled success lined up for your destiny. I believe this year will be a turnaround year for you. It doesn't matter how you start, it matters how you finish. I declare it's going to be a year of breakthrough for you. I declare you will never be the same and your latter will be greater than your former. I call forth restoration in your life. I believe that the place of greatness you imagine for yourself; you belonged there before you got there. I speak life over every dead and desolate that has held you back. I release peace, hope and faith into the atmosphere for you right where you are at. Now together, let's turn the

page.

CHAPTER ONE

TURN THE PAGE ON REJECTION AND DEVASTATION

Rejection is painful. It does not discriminate. Rejection is the enemy's way of making you feel devalued. It is his weak attempt to get you off track. Rejection can be felt in childhood and adulthood. Rejection can lead to devastation. It is how we manage rejection that will determine our ability to overcome the devastation. Experiencing rejection and devastation hurts deeply. Once you have moved past it, revisiting a memory can evoke emotions you would rather keep buried. I challenge you today to not bury the pain, rather confront it. I know confrontation is uncomfortable but it is possible. You were born for greatness not defeat. You have the strength built in you to overcome the pain of yesterday. Decide today, that you will begin to turn the page and move forward.

Allow me to introduce you to the R4 methodology that has set thousands on course to living a life free from the weight of rejection, devastation, fear, setbacks, labels and low self-esteem. Maybe, you deal with unforgiveness, lack, settling, quitting or being inconsistent. Whatever your struggle, God wants you to live a life of freedom. God loves you so much. He wants you to enjoy life not endure it. He wants you to thrive not just survive. All that you have been through has been a process that will deliver evidence-based results, proving God's miracle working power in and through your life.

God is the President and CEO of the universe. He is the author and finisher of our faith. God is the beginning and the end. He is the creator of mass and matter. You are important to Him. You were created with purpose. He values you and placed gifts inside of you that line up with your destiny. You have the power and strength in you and behind you, to see destiny and purpose collide, positioning you into the greatness you were destined for.

I remember the day the Lord showed me R4. It was a quite weekday morning; I was on the Monreal ranch in South Austin, surrounded by acres of nature. I was studying the Word at a small table in the guest-house as I prepared for an upcoming conference. It was at that moment when the Lord dropped in my spirit four powerful words: Release, Remove, Restore and Re-deem. I call it the R4 methodology.

R4 consists of four distinct components. Let's begin with release. Release occurs the moment you surrender the situation and your issue. The moment you truly, yet simply, let go of the hurt, disappointment, anger, frustration and the overall emotions tied to the memory replaying the rejection. Rejection leads to devastation. Devastation can be experienced through crushing moments of disappointment and defeat. Sometimes things happen that are completely over-whelming and equally unjust. We unintentionally end up carrying a load God

> *"Quit replaying the pain of yesterday. It is time to turn the page."*

never intended us to carry. As difficult as the situation may have been, it is time to turn the page. Quit replay-ing the pain of yesterday. God wants to heal the wounded areas of your life. God has brighter days ahead for you. I call forth the seeds of greatness in you. I speak healing to your spirit, soul and body. You were created to do the extraordinary. The enemy cannot steal

the promises God has placed over your life.

There was a man in the bible named Moses.

When Moses was a baby, the Pharaoh of the land gave

a decree that males two years and under were to be

killed. Imagine the grief his mother felt when she heard

that order from the leader of her land. To have your

newborn ordered to death was devastating. Moses fell

under the umbrella order to be killed as a child. God

"Pressure is not always wanted but it produces the promise." designed him to be a deliverer of his people. What a dilemma! How would this work? Talk about creativity in navigating the surviv-

al of a male child under a decree of death. Now is a

good time to point out that nothing is impossible for

God. When the pressure of what we are facing seems

insurmountable, remember the purpose for your life requires process and preparation. There is pressure in the process. Pressure is not always wanted but it can produce the promise. Sometimes, the pressures we experience are not even God sent; they are straight up attacks from the enemy. But know this; God will work all things together for your good. You will not fail, turn the page today.

The enemy had a plan to kill Moses. God had a plan that trumped the enemy and utilized the greatest system in the land to raise-up and train Moses. God is the master orchestrator and can simplify complicated situations. One day, Moses' mother decided she could no longer hide Moses. She had been hiding him since birth due to the decree issued in the land to kill all males under two years old. One day, she sent him down the river in a sealed and secure basket. She stood in faith in the midst of heartache and her hope kept her moving forward. As the basket with Moses floated down the river, it was seen, retrieved and brought before Pharaoh's daughter.   Pharaoh's daughter was aware of her father's decree but decided to keep Moses.

"Our obstacles, misfortune and heartache do not disqualify us from fulfilling purpose."

From that day forward Moses was raised in Pharaoh's house as an Egyptian. Although he was a Hebrew and all of the Hebrew people were slaves; Moses never really made the connection until the time had come for destiny and purpose to collide. Our obstacles, misfortune and heartache do not disqualify us from fulfilling purpose. God used Pharaoh's house, an influential and powerful place to educate, clothe, feed, and train the same man

who would come back and deliver the Hebrews.

The promise and potential inside of you cannot

lay dormant and secret for long. The dream you were

born with cannot remain buried, covered and hidden.

The promises inside of you are larger than the opposi-

tion you have experienced and stronger than the voices

of the enemies that surround you. You must turn the

> *"You may think and feel you have been down the wrong road and it has drifted you from your purpose and promise. But that road has shielded you, fed you, educated you and prepared you for your destiny."*

page. Moses' mother released her promise by faith. Her son was her promise. God was orchestrating his life's events. For forty years, Moses was trained, clothed, educated

and protected. You think you have missed opportunities, you think you have lost and you are in your final chapters of life; but you are closer than you can imagine to fulfilling destiny. Israel thought it was over. They had been enslaved for almost four hundred years. Israel had resigned. They were tired and worn out, but God said, "Your deliverer has come." You may think and feel you have been down the wrong road and it has drifted you from your purpose and promise. But that road has shielded you, fed you, educated you and prepared you for your destiny. Just as God was grooming Moses to deliver his people, God has been preparing you. God is going to use you to deliver others.

> *"You were called to impact, influence and inspire those around you."*

You were called to impact, influence and inspire those around you. As his life story continued to unfold he had to step into the destiny God called him into, even though he was unfamiliar with what the future would hold. Stepping into your purpose is a step of faith. Some of you have been afraid to step into the destiny God has called you to. It's time to turn the page.

Release generates freedom. Do not be afraid to release and surrender your situation to God. He can handle it. When you release the weight that has been bearing down on you, you will notice you have a new ability to lean on him. Sometimes we attempt to believe that we are strong in our own strength and can withstand the pressure. You can withstand the pressure however; it is through God's strength. It is him we need to lean on. You are strong in the power of God's might.

There is a difference between standing strong and becoming hardhearted. Have you ever met someone who was hardhearted? It's easy to become hardhearted in the journey of life, but releasing the obstacles to God allows you to focus on strength and standing strong. In South Texas, there is a port called The Port of Corpus Christi. This port brings in huge oil tankers and cleans them out. They may stay there for six to eight months. The objective is not to stay docked, but to allow the tanker to extract all of the oil residue that was held in the tankers. So when they go back out, they will not have corrosion build up and corrupt the new oil being loaded.

So it is with us, we have to release the built up residue of yesterday's problems and make room for the promises God has in store for you. God has goodness and favor waiting to be deposited in your life. Understand, you were not meant to walk this road alone. God is with you. His burden is easy and his yoke is light.

The amalgamations of our life experiences, the good,

the bad and the ugly; God will use it. He can make a

sweet fragrance out of a hodgepodge of mess. God

wants you to know that it is not over! It is not too late.

Your new beginning is on the other side.

       I was having lunch with a successful couple one

afternoon and they shared an inspiring story with me.

This couple had been married for 15 years and had their

share of trials through life. Eric and Marissa were the

typical young couple when they first married. They

were young, in love, hopeful and sweetly naïve in so

many ways. They were blessed with the opportunity to

purchase their first home during their engagement and

spent their first night as a married couple in it prior to

leaving for their honeymoon. The new house was small,

cozy, had a gazebo in the back, centrally located within the city, recently upgraded, remodeled and most importantly it was theirs. It was their first major investment. Married life was off to a great start. Within the first two years of marriage, the organization Eric was working for fell upon difficult times. The financial hardship resulted in a reduction in force, which impacted Eric's continued employment. He searched for employment high and low but could not solidify anything. Soon, they began to experience strain on their personal finances. Their ability to stay committed to their financial obligations was in a crisis status. They reduced everything around but after months of stress, pressure and failure to meet mortgage obligations, their home went into foreclosure. The reality of foreclosure was devastating. It crushed their spirit and dampened their outlook. If there was a point they felt at the bottom of the barrel of life, it was right then. Their faith was shot and officially shipwrecked. You could definitely categorize that as a low point. Looking back, they now know they could have done so many things differently. They quickly became the talk of their social circles. As if they were not already feeling rejected and devastated, public commentary started pouring in. Everyone had an opinion. There was even a close relative that said, "They didn't deserve the house in the first place." The church wasn't so welcoming and as they turned to the house of God to seek direction on next steps, stares and whispers could be observed.

They moved in with Eric's parents for a few months to get back on their feet. That was not easy either. Although, they felt they were at rock bottom, they did not give up. There was a hope stirring inside, assuring them better days laid ahead. There is an old saying "You can't keep a good man down and crème always rises to the top." Together, they cultivated a plan and with God's help they were in another house five months later. They never again went through a similar situation but nevertheless, those short few months impacted them for quite some time. As they began to rebuild, they chose to release the situation to God and allow Him to remove the pain, restore what was lost and redeem them to the place God always intended them to be. It was not an overnight process but they decided to turn the page. They decided to focus on the future not the past. They focused on what they could turn around and how they could make impact instead of dwelling on regret and allowing bitterness to settle in.

Eric and Marissa released the unanswered questions, hurt, disappointment, anger, frustration, and learned from the experience. Today, over a decade later, they live in a beautiful home, in a great community with wonderful people. They both have successful careers and are well established. They said they felt like that season was a lifetime ago. Maybe today you are walking through a season where you have experienced significant loss in your life. There are better days ahead for your journey of life. I asked Eric what was the turning point? How did you both move past the devastation associated with loss? How did you get out of a shipwrecked state and get your faith back on track? It was one move, they turned the page.

Eric shared how one day, as he was reading the Bible reflecting on scripture, he came across a chapter in the Old Testament, where God commanded Israel to bury the deceased outside of the city. The purpose was so they could live without passing by the grave to constantly remind them of the past. That process really moved Eric. He shared it with Marissa and together they decided it was time to move on. This financial catastrophe impacted them long enough. They would not allow one negative situation to define them. They sat together at the kitchen table, cried and created a list of every hurt and pain from the event, including words that were spoken to them and took a trip approximately, forty-five miles out of town. They pulled over on an old, secluded dirt road, got out of the car, popped open the truck, took out a shovel and began to dig a shallow hole. They buried the list of hurts as a sign and a symbol of moving forward and forgetting what was behind. I do not recommend digging a hole on public or private property these days. It might be better to create your list and throw in the fireplace but for the sake of full disclosure, that day; they turned the page on humiliation, hurt, shame and resentment.

What do you need to release in your life? There is hope for tomorrow. Your life is worth living. Don't allow one situation or tragedy to define your future, turn the page today on rejection and devastation. Running your race to fulfill your purpose will take you to places you have never dreamed of because they are places God already had planned for you. They released their pain, God removed the sting of devastation, restored and redeemed their finances.

A middle aged woman named Isabella shared a story with my wife Veronica about love from her younger days. Isabella's story is common because it happens to many young college girls, but her story is also unique because it showed how God healed her heart as she turned the page. Isabella was in love with Frankie. Frankie was tall, dark and handsome. He had a sweet personality, completely swept Isabella off of her feet and Frankie was a Christian. Isabella felt she hit the jackpot with Frankie. Frankie seemed to be everything Isabella wanted in a man. Isabella would melt every time she would hear him sing or minister. Frankie was different than the other men Isabella had dated. The men she dated previously were in gangs, involved in crime and drug ventures. None of them compared to what she saw in Frankie. When she met Frankie she thought she had finally found "the one." Isabella and

Frankie had fun together every moment they could,

they had a special bond, dreamed together about the

future and both had a load of potential as a couple.

One day Isabella got a call from a stranger. Isa-

bella was unsure of how this person reached her but this

person began to disclose the countless hours they had

been spending with Frankie. The stranger began sharing

special moments they shared with Frankie that were

intimate. Isabella was in pure disbelief but in her heart

felt these stories were true. All of the alleged timetables

matched up. Isabella quickly hung up the phone and

called Frankie. She questioned Frankie and sure

enough, Frankie had been seeing someone else. Isabella

felt rejected as a woman, she felt she was not good

enough and while every ounce of her wished it was a bad dream, it was not.

Isabella began being harassed. Overtime, she was able to distance herself and start over with a new circle of friends. Isabella questioned everything she knew about relationships for some time. Her heart was broken. The man she loved was in love with someone else. This devastation bred distrust in men. For two years, Isabella took a break from dating. She focused on her relationship with the Lord and worked on finishing college, and deciding on a career. One day while at church she met a stunning young man who took her breath away. Her prior experience caused her to be cautious but as she began to get to know this young man her heart began to trust again. Her heart could trust again, because she turned the page on the old relationship. Turning the page brings healing. To complicate

life after successfully moving on, Isabella received a

random call at work. Isabella had been dating Matthew,

the new young man in her life for a little over a year.

They were thinking about marriage and Frankie was a

thing of the past. One day, answering the phone at

work, three years after the Frankie situation, she heard

his voice. Frankie broke up with the one he dumped

Isabella for and was with a new girl named Jezlynn for

approximately a year up to that point. Frankie decided

he was going to marry Jezlynn. Isabella was completely

unaware of his intentions as she had moved on with her

life. Frankie said as Isabella was in shock to hear his

voice, "I heard you are dating Matthew and it's getting

serious, do you love him?" Isabella was shocked to

have received the call. She felt compelled to dig deep

34

and ask herself if what she was experiencing was truly love. Remember, she had loved Frankie at one time. Had she truly moved forward or was this just a cover because she was still sunk, hook, line and sinker for Frankie? Isabella felt old emotions arise, simply hearing his voice on the phone. As she and Frankie chatted, she realized Frankie was planning to marry Jezlynn within a few short weeks. Frankie told Isabella he would call off the wedding if she didn't love Matthew and together he and Isabella could build a wonderful life together. After a long pause, she said, "No Frankie, I love Matthew." She decided to not only turn the page, but also sever the connection they once had. She moved forward and today she and Matthew have been married almost 20 years. God has new beginnings in store for you as you turn the page on love. As you release unhealthy relationships, God will remove the emotion associated with the ties and he will restore and redeem your love life with someone who he predestined and ordained you to be with. God cares about your love life.

You cannot give up. Sometimes people are tempted to settle along life's journey as hiccups are encountered along the road. Keep focused on God's plan for your life. Put your work in and lean on his strength and not your own. Had Isabella, Eric and Marissa not released the pain of the past they could not focus on the promises of tomorrow.

The next R4 step is remove. My good friend, Pastor Servando Ozuna, shared a simple but profound story with me about a child who lived in a foreign country and got a splinter lodged in his foot. Every day, his parents would remind him not to walk around the house without his shoes. Their floors were wooden and had not been sanded down. Daily this child would heed his parent's instruction. It became routine and habit. One day, he decided he would disregard the advice and walk around with bare feet. As expected, a splinter became deeply lodged in his foot. It hurt, but he ignored the pain. He continued to play, but sensitivity was building up around the place of impact. The splinter eventually became so infected he developed a limp. His parents asked, "Son, why are you limping?" At first he lied. As the parents continued to probe, he eventually explained what happened. His parents immediately removed the splinter. The pain experienced during the removal was temporary as the issue was confronted. The pain experienced from holding on was more severe and caused infection. As soon as the splinter was removed, the healing process began. They applied medication and soon, his foot was completely normal. Sometimes we hold onto situations that cause infections because we do not want to confront them. I promise you the pain of confrontation is not as difficult as the pain of walking around with an infection. When you release the splinters in your life, God is able to move in, remove the pain and heal the infection.

The pain of yesterday does not compare to the promise of tomorrow. Turning the page activates healing. When you turn the page you are saying good-bye to the hurt of yesterday and hello to the promises of tomorrow.

> *"The pain of yesterday does not compare to the promise of tomorrow."*

I want you to imagine, a healthy, strong, athletic person in your mind. This person has defined muscle,

they can run fast, drive hard and have nothing that will
get in the way or hold them back from pursuing their
goal. Now imagine with me, they tie a rope around their
waist and the other end of the rope is tied around an oak
tree. The rope signifies hurt, rejections, betrayal and
disappointments. Every-time they take off to run, they
are held back. One may think it's the oak tree that has
anchored roots is holding them back. However, it is the
rope that is holding them back. As soon as you cut the
rope or they allow it to drop to their ankles, they
experience freedom. As you allow God to remove
ropes in your life, you begin to experience the freedom
to run and walk again. You were born for greatness.
You can't allow the ropes of life to tie you to a station-
ary tree, anchored in one place. You must break free
and turn the page. You were created to run a race. You

were created to win and not be held back. God's plan
for your life is to give you hope and a successful future.
Turn the page today.

The next R4 process is restore. My grandfather,
Virgil Tucker, played the trumpet. He was an amazing
man and accomplished musician. Grandpa Tucker
traveled as a full-time minister and played with the best
of the best. You could find him on a national stage or in
an old country church. He loved the Lord and he found
great joy as he would sing, write music, preach and
teach; all on a professional level. I remember as a child,
one visit where Grandpa Tucker came over, he was up
in age and nearing his time to go home to be with Jesus.
He took his trumpet out, began taking it apart, intended
to clean it and put it back together as he had done
hundreds of times before. Only this time, he was unable

to put it back together. My mom told him not to worry about it; she would take the trumpet to the music shop and a master level restorer would put it back together. She did and that year my grandpa passed away. She has the trumpet to this day and it's in a restored condition. Grandpa Tucker frequently said "Glue and tape always work great!" Some of you can no longer function with the broken pieces in your heart. Some broken pieces come from pain experienced on a secondary level. Maybe it was a tragedy that happened to your child. Maybe it was an illness that attacked your spouse or sibling and broke your heart. All of us appear whole externally, but as the trumpet was taken apart, it took a master level professional to put it back together. As life's trials tear you apart, I want you to know God is here and ready to put you back together again. He understands every facet of your life, including the parts you do not share with others. He has been waiting on you to turn the page. Are you ready? Today is your day for healing. Today is your day to move forward. Today is your day to experience new beginnings. Today is your day to be restored.

Say this prayer with me: "God, all of me belongs to all of you. Take every broken piece and make me whole. Restore me. I love you Lord. I trust that you are in control and my later day will be greater than my most recent experiences."

The Scripture tells us in Isaiah 61:3 (NLT):

"To all who mourn in Israel, he will give a crown of beauty for ashes, a joyous blessing instead of mourning, festive praise instead of despair, in their righteousness, they will be like great oaks that the LORD has planted

for his own glory." God's restoration is greater than you
can imagine.

When God restores, He will accelerate your life
and put you where you were predestined to be. The
bible tells us He will restore to you the years that the
locusts have eaten, the cankerworm, the caterpillar, and
the palmerworm. God is in the business of restoration.
In the original Hebrew, according to the Strong's
concordance, the word locust means sudden disappearance, and insignificance. Strong's also shows the
Hebrew word for cankerworm as "Yehlek" and it
means a young locust and early stage of development.
God was saying I will restore the early years of your
life that the enemy robbed from you. Whatever happened, God will restore the early developments of life.
You believe time has been lost, innocence violated,

43

hope destroyed, love betrayed, and your faith shipwrecked; God will restore.

The next word is caterpillar; the Strong's
concordance explains that it means to eat away. God
will restore what has eaten away at life. If you have
ever seen termites, they take small bites out of solid
wood. The wood becomes worn down and needs
replacement after the extermination of the termites. God
wants you to know He will restore what has been worn
down and out in your life. The negative words spoken,
the extra labor, the confidence the enemy has eaten at.
God will restore! Restoration begins when we turn the
page.

The Strong's concordance shows the Hebrew
word for palmerworm is "gazam" and it means "to
devour." When something is devoured, there is nothing

left. The very thing that set out to destroy you, God will use to cultivate you. God will restore the empty places of your life. Do not give up! God will restore what has been taken from you. What others have devalued and called insignificant, God calls significant. Allow the restoration process to begin.

The Last R4 is redeem. The redemption process of life is always greater than the offense, and what has occurred. There was a man by the name of Job in the bible. He was a faithful servant who lost his family, experienced financial devastation and whose faith was tested. He was in true need of redemption. The bible says that when it was all said and done, God redeemed his life with more than Job could imagine. What would have taken years, God did in exponential time. God redeemed Job's name, integrity and character. Some of you today, need God to redeem some areas of your life.

I am here to tell you He is ready! God is ready for you

to turn the page.

A PRAYER

Heavenly Father, I release the rejection and devastation I have experienced. I know it is not your will for me to walk around defeated. Remove the pain and restore my life. I turn the page today. I declare by faith you make me whole. I declare I am healed emotionally and walking in divine restoration. I thank you I am free to be me. In Jesus name; amen

CHAPTER 2
TURN THE PAGE ON FEAR AND SETBACKS

As a child I grew up watching a television series called, "The Incredible Hulk." I remember thinking what would I do if the Hulk came out of the television set? It sounds funny now, but it was a fear as a seven year old boy. I played out different scenarios in my mind and tried to figure out what I would do if the big green guy came out of the television set. I remember some days watching the show while sitting on my couch but as soon as David Banner began turning into the big, green hulk, I would stand up and get in a defensive stance.

In reality, the big, green hulk would not come out of the television set to fight me. However, my fear played various scenarios in my mind. I outgrew it as I matured and recognized what I feared was not possible. Today, I enjoy watching the show with my two boys. I look back and laugh but I want you to think about how fear can torment you. It can impact and impair you from enjoying life. Fear can build on fear. I not only was afraid of being engaged in a fight with the Hulk in my parent's living room, I was afraid of destroying furniture or tearing down a wall while knocking out the front door. My parents would have freaked out! This was all **f**alse **e**vidence **a**ppearing **r**eal.

Fear can hold you back from pursuing the dreams God placed in your heart. Fear can incarcerate you. Fear can cause anxiety. Fear can drive panic attacks. Fear is something you need to manage and control. Fear can breed intimidation.

If you have been dealing with fear in different areas of your life, I invite you to step out and be coura-geous. You have more courage inside of you than you think. You were born to be more than a conqueror. You were equipped and destined to achieve great results in life. You were born to have victory over the opposition you face. It is time to stand and move. It is the movers and shakers of this nation who make a difference. There is a still small voice inside of you, telling you to step out in faith. That is the unction of the Holy Spirit.

You may have a new job, work in a new department or a new level of the organization and while you are excited you may equally be nervous and uneasy inside.

Declare over your life, no weapon formed against you will prosper. Declare you are more than a conqueror through Christ Jesus. Declare you were born to be the head and not the tail. Declare you are going over and not under. Declare that favor is coming your way and with

God watching over his promises, doors are opening for you. Turn the page on fear and setbacks.

I know a woman named Heather. Heather lost her father as a little girl. When he passed away her heart was shattered into pieces. She was loved by her remaining parent and siblings but unintentionally pushed those outside of that circle who wanted to get close to her away. She didn't realize she was doing this; it was an unintentional result of the experience from her father passing away at an early age. When Heather matured and was ready to date, relationships were a challenge because she remained guarded, determined to not allow another great loss in her life. Heather did not fear love, she feared loss. One day she made the decision to let the man she wanted to marry past those guarded emotions. Heather took a chance on love and risked the possibility of loss. She chose to confront her fear and not allow it to control her. Today, this couple has a strong and vibrant marriage. Imagine if she would not have moved past fear. Heather stepped out of her comfort zone. Heather told her mind what to think. Heather took authority over negative thoughts. Heather cast down vain imaginations that her husband would die at an early age. She refused to fear and instead stood in faith. She believed that everything was going to work out. Heather has been married now for 17 years.

Johnny dreamed of being an attorney from a young age. Life was rough growing up as his family struggled financially. The dream of becoming an attorney came with the expense of college. Being raised with only one parent, college seemed out of reach. His mother never discouraged him but friends did. Some friends said college would take too long, four years,

plus grad school. Other friends said it would be too

expensive and not an economically sound decision for

his family. Other friends simply thought he should be a

teacher or another career they found compelling and

stable. When Johnny finished high school, he got a job

and began his academic journey at a local community

college. Johnny went with what the crowd said, with

what society implied, not with what was planted in his

heart. He never pursued being an attorney and for

almost 20 years, struggled with the regret of not

pursuing his dream. God places dreams in our heart for

a purpose. Johnny landed good jobs after college.

Johnny was happily married, a great father to his

children but something was missing deep down inside.

He buried it over the years, but that was the desire to go

to law school and become an attorney. Returning to

school at this stage in life would require sacrifice. The

family would need to reprioritize and reposition

schedules and responsibilities. Together, the family

pulled together to fulfill a lifelong dream. Today

> *"God has not called you to live a mediocre life; he's called you to fulfill purpose."*

Johnny has returned to school

and is on a journey to be an

attorney. Friends, it is never

too late. Go after what God put

in your heart. It may have taken you fifteen years to get

over a setback but the point is you are moving forward

and not settling. You got this! Go get it! God has not

called you to live a mediocre life; He's called you to

fulfill purpose. The opinions of others do not define

who you are and neither should they carry enough

weight to detour you from your destiny. What has God

placed on your heart that you need to pick back up? Are

you ready to turn the page?

This woman I know in her thirty's suffered from

anxiety. She was a successful executive who had a

traumatic experience in her twenties. Any time, any

situation even remotely resembled the trauma she

experienced she would get shortness of breath, feel heat

up and down her body and even though she was in a

completely different environment, completely different

circumstance, it wasn't something she couldn't easily

shake off. She would get light headed, her heart would

race and she would be completely overwhelmed. It was

almost sixteen years after the traumatic experience

before she came to the realization that what had

happened in her twenties was not likely to occur again.

She had to accept that while it could happen again and

it would be horrible, she had to decide to not live with the fear that set deep down inside underneath the joys of life. This fear was buried. One day, she decided she would not be imprisoned by those emotions, by the triggers that caused her body to physiologically tense up and react as it did. This fear was real for her. She decided to not allow this experience to establish a monument in her life that would serve as a barrier continually causing setbacks. She renews her mind with positive thoughts daily. She takes practical actions to ensure there is not a re-occurrence. I want to emphasis how she takes authority over her thoughts. She lines her thoughts up with reality and the positive potential of a situation not the fearful side of a situation. The moment she feels a panic attack trying to arise, she immediately pauses, takes several deep breaths and begins telling herself, "Everything is going to be okay." She rehearses Scriptures in her mind till they enter her heart and take over her emotions. She does not allow the current situation to trigger the raw release of negative streams of negative possibilities. Some of her favorite morning rehearsals are:

- No weapon formed against me shall prosper. (Is: 54:17)

- I am more than a conqueror. (Romans 8:27)

- My latter will be greater than my former. (Haggai 2:9)

- God is with me everywhere I go. (Jeremiah 23:23-24)

- God has plans to prosper me not harm me. (Jeremiah 29:11)

- God is the God of the impossible. (Mark 9:23)

- God is working things together for my good. (Romans 8:28)

- God has made me the head and not the tail. I am going over obstacles not getting stuck in front of them. (Deuteronomy 28:13)

- God has not given me a spirit of fear but of power, love and sound mind. (2 Timothy 1:7)

- This will not come upon me a second time. (Nahum 1:9)

She continues to rationalize in her mind that present day circumstances do not equate to the traumatic experience she once went through. She refuses to live in fear. It's a fight every day, but that is the key, she is fighting forward. She continues to walk forward and find peace.

There is a passage of scripture found in Ruth 3:18 (NLT), where Naomi, tells Ruth, "Just be patient, my daughter, until we hear what happens. The man won't rest until he has settled things today." Naomi was explaining to Ruth, the setback and fear of uncertainty in life was about to turn around. You see, in the scripture you will find the concepts of standing still and sitting still. While you are standing still, it is as if you are on standby and ready to move in an instant.

Sitting still is a different approach. Sitting still means you are in a posture of learning and hearing instructions. Sitting still, is a more passive method. Isaiah 40:31 (KJV) "But they that wait upon the Lord shall renew their strength; they shall mount up with wings as eagles; they shall run, and not be weary; and they shall walk, and not faint." Mounting means to increase in amount, to place, fix, or fasten in proper support. Eagle's wings are strong and can even reach the span of eight feet long with the ability to soar into the sky toward the sun with the strength as a horse. When we are mounting up with wings as an eagle, we are being prepared to increase in our spiritual walk, physical health, relationships, economic situations, and every other area of our lives. Although you may be in a period of waiting, this season in your life God is renewing your strength, mounting you up with wings as an eagle, and causing you not to be weary of the journey as you are running and walking. This season is a place of development and in it, He is teaching you endurance. God needs us to be able to withstand the pressure that comes with our call and turn the page on fear and setbacks.

Remember Joseph from the Old Testament? Joseph is one of my favorite men in the bible. He went through so much yet went so far. He experienced setbacks and God turned them into set ups. Joseph was misunderstood; his character was assassinated. When you think worse could not come upon a person, it did for Joseph and yet somehow, through it all, he pulled through. Joseph refused to allow the trails of life and attacks of the enemy to bury him. He fought his way to victory. Joseph's refusal to submit to the derailments of life was the beginning of his promotion. In spite of his circumstances, he kept focused on God's plan for his life. Joseph understood in order to make it through he would need to continually turn the page. After Joseph was sold in slavery to the Ishmaelites; they went to Egypt and sold him again.

When you face tragedy and you can't seem to catch your breath before another calamity strikes, you have to know deep down on the inside that this too shall

pass. Each time, Joseph turned the page. It was hard.

There were tears and loads of raw emotions. Each time

he would process, compartmentalize and set out to

make a negative situation better.

　　After he was sold, a man by the name of Poti-

phar bought him. Potiphar was the Captain of the palace

guards. Joseph worked for Potiphar. Joseph was a loyal

man. He was handsome, well respected and a trusted

employee. Potiphar's wife was attracted to Joseph. So

much so, she wanted to have sexual relations with him.

Joseph refused the offer. While he was doing the right

thing by refusing the offer, she did not take the rejec-

tion well. As a matter of fact, she staged the scenario to

appear as though he attempted to sexually assault her.

Potiphar's wife lied. Potiphar's wife lie resulted in

prison time for Joseph. He was wrongly accused. In

today's society, in America, there would be due pro-

cess. However, although maybe not as extreme as

Joseph's situation we have all faced times where we

were wrongly accused, mistreated, lied about, the center

of gossip or some type of

injustice. Difficult people are

good for our development. The

> *"Difficult people are good for our development."*

enemy's goal was to ultimately destroy Joseph's life.

Joseph refused to submit to the destruction. His internal

resolve caused him to turn the page five different times

in life.

Turning the page does not have to be a onetime

event. The first time, Joseph had a dream. He was

excited to share it. He didn't understand what it fully

meant but as he reached out to those, closest to him, he

was rejected and despised. His dream was laughed at. Joseph was hurt but he turned the page.

Second, was when his father made him a coat of many colors and Joseph had another dream. He again was rejected only this time, not just from his brothers but also his father. Rejection from a father is difficult to bounce back from. Joseph turned the page.

Third, Joseph was sold into slavery. How many times have we felt sold out? Betrayal hurts deep. Joseph turned the page.

Fourth, he was promoted then lied on and thrown back into prison. Have you ever received a promotion and immediately you realize you are in a new tank with sharks. Not everyone wants to celebrate you. Joseph turned the page.

Fifth, this was significant because Joseph was catapulted from prison to the palace, literally. You see Joseph shared a prison cell with Pharaoh's cup bearer and butler. The cup bearer and butler both had a dream. Joseph interpreted the dream and it came to pass, just as it was interpreted. Once the cup bearer resumed his position in the palace, Joseph asked the cup bearer not to forget about him. At the onset, he forgot about Joseph; always seemed like Joseph couldn't win. He was a good guy who was coming in last. However, two years later, Pharaoh had a dream and the cup bearer was reminded of Joseph and his accuracy in interpreting dreams. Joseph was called to appear before Pharaoh and he interpreted the dream. Joseph's gift to interpret dreams was still on point. Regardless of what you have been through in life, God has gifts and talents in you

that other people need. The opposition you have

> *"Regardless of what you have been through in life, God has gifts and talents in you that other people need."*

encountered, the tragedy you

have experienced, the pain

you have suffered, does not

disqualify you from becoming

your best version of you. God equipped you to over-

come. We set our own limitations. I want you to

purpose in your heart that you are going to turn the

page. You must be the loudest voice and decide today

that you are moving forward. Pharaoh promoted Joseph

to be second in command. Your promotion awaits you!

Your place of purpose still has your name on it and is

waiting for your occupancy! Joseph turned the page

releasing his pain, regret, all the why's, should have,

could have and would have's. Joseph decided he was

not going to live a life living in fear nor dwelling on

setbacks. Joseph married into a family that would be

equivalent to modern day billionaires.

I invite you to study the life of Joseph. God ac-

celerated his life and redeemed the time. You may feel

it's too late in life for God to redeem the time. It is not

too late. What would have taken a lifetime to achieve,

God did for Joseph in one day. There are many of you

out there, who have been short changed and just like

Joseph, it seems like it will take a lifetime to get ahead.

God can do more than we can ask, think or imagine.

When you are pursing your dreams, the enemy will

always attempt to derail you and cause delays but your

divine destiny awaits you! II Corinthians 5:7 (NLT)

"We walk by faith, not by sight."

Have you ever driven in a severe rain storm? You move the windshield wipers to go faster and they are going as fast as they can, yet it seems like the rain is obscuring your vision. When it's dark, it compounds the complexity of seeing. When you know the road, it's easier to stay the course. When you do not know the road, you either need to pull over or drive at an extremely safe and slower speed. The road of life is easier to navigate when you depend on the word of God as your light and navigation system. His directions will not fail you.

There was a man in the bible by the name of Noah. Noah's story can be found in the book of Genesis. He was a man of extreme faith. He was directed by the Lord to build an ark. That sounds simple, but you must understand the context surrounding the Lords direction. To begin, an ark is not a simple boat to take out on the lake or go deep sea fishing. An ark is huge. The ark Noah was asked to build was approximately four hundred and fifty feet long, seventy-five feet wide and forty-five feet high in modern translation. It is important to note that when Noah was asked to build the ark, it had not rained in over one hundred years. Sometimes in life we encounter tasks that seem impossible to achieve but they are part of us reaching our destiny. Noah built the ark. Noah saved his family and animals as God designed. You may be reading this book and have always known you were destined to own your business but you have listed to the opposition. Do not allow the option of failure to outweigh the possibility of success. Be Noah. Do it even though it hasn't rained in one hundred years. Do it even though you

have never owned a business

before. Do it even if you did

own a business and it failed.

What God has promised for

> *"Do not allow the option of failure to out-weigh the possibility of success."*

you is yours. We have to do the practical and go after it.

Maybe you have been contemplating running for office

but you feel you did not come from the political pedi-

gree to do so. Be Noah, you can do it. Noah did not

have a university to enroll into to figure out the prag-

matics of nautical construction or engineering. Did you

know that when Jesus started his ministry many of the

Pharisees, Sadducees and other Jews did not believe in

Him or accept Him as the Son of God? God always

zooms in on our potential; He positions us to reach the

promise, while the enemy zooms in on our failures. As

Noah stepped out in
faith, God supplied. As
Noah did the practical,
God did the providen-

> *"God always
> zooms in on our
> potential; he
> positions us to
> reach the promise"*

tial. Noah was faithful to build in spite of no rain and in

spite of no clouds. Noah believed God and God counted

him faithful. The component that kept Noah going was

the word God had spoken to him. Is there a promise

God has whispered into your heart. What is it? How

will you step out and build? How will you move past

fear and setbacks? How will turn the page? Today is

your day.

I know of a successful businessman named Vi-

cente. Vicente was a strong community leader, an

active member of his church, political contributor, solid

family man and sound decision maker. Professionals

from all walks of life would seek out his wisdom. The

Lord had blessed him financially and with such bless-

ings, he had a giving heart. An opportunity came up to

join a group of businessmen on several projects. These

projects would yield great financial gain. Vicente had

underlying reservations but was unsure because all the

details seemed like a win/win situation. Vicente and his

wife prayed about it, his wife felt the same reservations.

The business proposal was so compelling they sought

counsel from a trusted source. This trusted source did

not pray about the opportunity he simply saw how

much the project would yield, the low risks involved

and financial increase Vicente and his family would

experience. Vicente moved forward and engaged in the

business deal. The first year was great. The second year

was okay however, the water was beginning to get

murky after first quarter, year two. Soon thereafter, lawsuit after lawsuit hit. It was a terrible time for this family. Their business assets were significantly diminished. They were forced to sell their luxurious home and forfeit that lifestyle. He eventually had to relocate his business outside of the city because his reputation was ripped to shreds locally. This family was devastated. They felt like they experienced more than a setback but a literal near death. The emotional toll this took on the marriage relationship, the relationship between the children, relocating a business, employees, housing and all of the logistics was extreme. Through it all, Vicente refused to lose hope. Although it was very small, each day as the sun would come up, his hope would increase and faith would be strengthened. It has taken Vicente more than a decade to get back on his feet. Sometimes situations can throw us so off course and we lose focus.

However, you cannot forget the promise you once held

in your heart. God is God in the good times and the bad

times. Vicente turned the page. He shared with me that

he had to turn the page multiple times through this

journey. Turning the page is essential if you plan to rise

back up to the top. As Vicente journey's back to the

top, he holds onto the scrip-

> *"If you can believe all things are possible unto him that believes."*
> Mark 9:23 (NLT)

ture found in Mark 9:23

(NLT). If you can believe all

things are possible unto him

that believes.

    After a setback, making a comeback requires a

positive attitude, a confession of faith and a determina-

tion for excellence. The emotional distress experienced

in a setback can seem disabling. Negative thoughts will

try to creep in and discourage you from believing the sun will shine again. In the scripture, found in Numbers, when the children of Israel sent their spies to Jericho to search out the Land, two came back with a report reflecting possibility; ten came back emphasizing the impossibility. One report focused on the size of the people, and inability to penetrate the city wall. To be exact, in Numbers 13:33, (NLT) they said "We are as grasshoppers in their sight." The walls of Jericho surrounding the city were so thick they would race chariots on them. Although, we may see the impossibilities of a situation or success

> *"Seeing life through the eyes of the Lord and His word causes us to not waiver and enjoy the life God has promised."*

can seem so far off, God is in our corner. He is our corner man and nothing is impossible with God. Caleb and Joshua were the spies with the positive reports.

Caleb said in Numbers 13:30 (NLT), "Let us go up at

once, for we are more than able to take the city." You

see, Caleb had already taken God at His word. He was

not denying the facts or difficulties, he simply decided

to speak by faith, believe by faith and act by faith.

Seeing life through the eyes of the Lord and His word

causes us to not waiver and enjoy the life God has

promised.

A PRAYER

Heavenly Father, I turn the page today on fear and setbacks. You said in your word that you have not given me a spirit of fear, but of power, love and a sound mind. I will not fear the future. I will not fear the past. You are with me. Thank you for using every setback I have experienced as a setup for your divine intervention and acceleration. I declare my mind is focused; my emotions are at peace and in line with the Word of God. Thank you for loving me and never failing me. I turn the page on fear and setbacks today. In Jesus name; amen.

CHAPTER 3

TURN THE PAGE ON LABELS AND LOW SELF-ESTEEM

In the late 90's when I was in high-school, if you wore a certain brand of jeans or if you wore a certain shirt, hung with a certain crowd, you were labeled a jock, skater, kicker, punk or prep. The brand you carried or style you wore was how others perceived you. After high-school, labeling was not over. When I went off to Bible College, you were labeled by which building your dorm room was in, what your major was, what fraternity or sorority you were part of, labels were all around. Same thing in the corporate world, people rank you by your title and level of responsibility. Some labels on your life are accurate. Other labels are not. The label you put on and respond to is what matters most.

Let me tell you about a man named Bartimaeus from the Bible. You can find his story in Mark 10:46-

52. His story is significant because in their society, if you were blind you were expected to wear a particular garment. This garment indicated you were blind, no one had to shout it from the mountain tops, it was just a given. Garments had significance in the bible days. There was certain attire for those with a royal background, priesthood, someone who was sickly or a beggar. For Bartimaeus, he fell in line with society's expectations. He wore the garment for the blind. When he heard Jesus was coming to town, he removed his garment by faith and followed after the one who could heal him. This was out of the box back then. Bartimaeus believed for a miracle and likewise acted on it. He was ready to turn the page. He was seeking out his healing. Bartimaeus wanted to be made whole. God

wants you to be whole. God is looking for you to take off the coat people have labeled you with.

Remember Joseph, the one whose father gave him a coat of distinction in the Bible; the coat of many colors? The reason that coat was so distinct is because customarily it was given to the oldest. However, Jacob, Joseph's father, gave it to him as the youngest. Jacob custom designed it for Joseph and it was an outward expression of his love for his son. The coat was costly to design and create. Joseph wearing the coat signified

> *"When Joseph's brothers stripped him of his garment, they did not strip him of his dream"*

that he would receive the birthright instead of his oldest brother Reuben. The coat of many colors was special. When Joseph's brothers stripped him of his garment, they did not strip him of his dream. God has a coat for you representing integrity, character, anointing and purpose. Some of you walk with this on; others are trying to find it. Refuse to identify with labels others give you and go with what the master of the universe says about you. You are specially made. You were hand crafted and custom built. No one, nowhere, compares to you. You are the apple of His eye. You are the pep in his step. God thinks of you and smiles.

The coat God designed for you was created to repel the labels and negative thoughts others try to project onto you. The coat God designed for you provides the endurance to weather a storm, to outlast challenges and overcome obstacles. The coat God designed for you contains grace, favor, mercy, encour-agement to make it through, healing for your soul, beauty for ashes, strength, gladness and peace. Put on the coat God has for you not the garment others have labeled you with.

God wants you to be free. He wants you to be free from what people think about you. Labels contribute to low self-esteem. When you suffer from low self-esteem you break free the moment you begin valuing yourself. God's voice is the ultimate voice that says you have been wonderfully made.

Growing up, my father, use to take us to the naval base to watch the annual "Air Show." We watched F-18 fighter jets perform special maneuvers. I was always in amazement of the Blue Angels and their performance. I remember one year, seeing one F-18 that went extremely slow. While it was going at an abnormally low speed, you could see the plane begin to vibrate. The crowd sighed because some F-18's have exploded due to the aircraft not possessing the capabil-

ity to navigate at a slow speed. F-18's are fighter jets,

they were designed for the battlefield, to carry bombs,

missiles, cannons and going slow is not part of the plan.

It can cause destruction. Just as a F-18 is designed to

be a fighter jet and on the battlefield, the coat God has

designed for you equally has a significant purpose. You

may have faced seasons where it feels like your plane is

going to explode, but you can turn the page and pick up

speed. As a matter of fact, some of you have been at a

potentially explosive level and it's time to turn the

page. Your best days are waiting for you on the other

side. The sun will rise again. Tomorrow is a new day.

You do not have to stay where others think you belong,

assign you or categorize you. You go after the dream

God has placed in your heart. I like to say it like this,

before you got there, you belong there! Before you

went after that promotion, God already knew you

belonged there. Those

property listings on that new

level, they belong to you.

> *"Before you got there, you belong there!"*

God knows the right clients, the right constituents,

stakeholders and community partners you need. I

declare favor is coming your way!

Some labels are passed down from generation to

generation with low self-esteem carrying on. I have a

friend who parents constantly struggled financially.

They couldn't win for losing; one tough break after

another. When this friend became an adult he shared

with me how he did not want to be like his parents. I

told him he didn't have to. He loved his parents so

much and it was hard to break away from the habits and

family way of doing things but they just were not

prosperous. The inability to save, move forward, and

succeed always seemed to plague them. One day, my

friend Alex decided he was going to turn the page. He

loved his family but he put a stop to the poverty, bad-

habits and fought his way to success. Today, Alex is

successful. Breaking the pattern of failure is possible.

Breaking the pattern of sin is possible. Instating the

pattern of redemption and restoration is possible. You

can instate and reinstate patterns by speaking the Word

of God. You have to gather a confession of faith. The

bible says in Proverbs 23:7 (KJV) ".....as a man

thinketh so is he." You must believe you are moving to

the next level and have actions to support your faith.

There was a man in the Bible by the name of

Abraham. Abraham was instructed by God to move to

the land of Canaan. Abraham was not called to live where he was currently residing. Transition was difficult but it was required to fulfill his purpose. Labels and low-self-esteem can keep us from transition, we need to push through. In order to be positioned for greatness, you must allow transition to occur. Abraham was called to impact globally. He could not do that where he was, he had to be stationed in Canaan. Are you stationed where you should be? Are you in position? Your coat of success is activated equally by your geographical location. Are you in the right place? Abraham left his country, his relatives, familiar places and everything he knew. When you grow, you must leave the old behind.

When Adam and Eve originally sinned in the garden, they attempted to cover their bodies with leaves. God covered them with animal skinned clothes.

Many times, others can try to cover us with leaves, these are labels. Or, we can try to cover ourselves with leaves, which is low self-esteem. Either way, God has a special garment for you. Your garment qualifies you for greatness, promotion, endurance, strength and joy. The benefits are limitless. God does not substitute, man does. Leaves were a substitute. God is the original. God's promises are so much greater than the life you are currently experiencing. Even if you are living on the promises of God, to know and grab hold that your future is greater than your past that is significant! If you are not living on the promises of God, I want you to know that He is only a prayer away. God will always forgive us and relocates us to the place of destiny.

Today, take off the coat of labels and low self-esteem. God has already measured your life. Your coat has all of God's promises hand woven in them. Your coat is threaded with love, courage, strength, wisdom, understanding, wealth, increase, patience, stamina, and favor. This coat only fits your life. When we take hold of the coat God has designed for us, we release the stress, struggle, and strain of life. Write this down: "God is not the author of confusion." God is not confused with your life. He is also not attempting to confuse your life either. My wife always says, "I am allergic to drama. Haters need to form a line to the left." What she is thinking is confusion will not be part of her life. She avoids drama like a plague. She cannot stand gossip; she is straightforward and does not allow opinions of others to put her in a box or corner. People and places may attempt to box you into a corner, but you can't allow their words to dress you for life's recital. God almighty who dressed the world with His words has dressed your life and labeled it outstanding, great and phenomenal! Even if that is not how you feel right now. Even if your circumstances around you are not outstanding, great and phenomenal, you have to speak those things that be not as though they were as the bible teaches in Romans 4:17. You see God has already marked you. You are God's masterpiece and nothing or anything can change that.

Your self-worth should not be what others have said; it should be what God has said about you. You

> "The labels today are not the benefits of the promises of tomorrow. Turn the page on labels."

were specifically tailored made for this season. Tailored made suits are exact and fit perfect. You are destined to fit into your purpose and prosper. The labels today are not the benefits of the promises of tomorrow. Turn the page on labels. Yes, it may be embarrassing to confront some of those labels and you might lose some friends but you will gain all of what God has pre-destined for your life. Our self-worth should never be because of what others have said it should always be because of what God has said.

When Adam and Eve sinned in the garden; they told God they were naked. God replied this profound, but simple statement "Who told you that?" I ask you today "Who told you that?" You know those phrases that play over and over in your mind? I take authority right now in the name of Jesus and speak freedom to your life! You are wonderfully made. You are breath taking. You are a great leader. You are a good parent. Don't allow labels to tell you differently. The enemy may have used people to attempt to sabotage your self-esteem, but you must remember what God has said about you. When you are taking a test, say what God has said, you are smart, intelligent, making the right decision, confess he is bringing back to your remembrance the right answers you have studied for. You might have been labeled the black sheep in the family, but God sees you as a great sheep. Your past is not an indicator of your future, God's Word is.

I encourage you today not to allow what others have spoken or what you have read to stop you from moving toward your goals

"Your past is not an indicator of your future, God's Word is."

and reaching your destiny. Your self-esteem is based upon what you value. If you value what God has said, then you will have a healthy self-esteem. Wake up every day and say I am making the right decisions, I am

a winner, I have your confidence, and I am highly

favored. I am overcoming and living victoriously. I am

whole, complete, and walking in divine health. Speak

and repeat what God has said you are. Remember who

told you that? Rehearse what God has said. Turn the

page today on labels and low self-esteem.

A PRAYER

Heavenly Father, I take the coat of labels off that others have put on me. I remove the coat I have put on myself with all of the negative self-talk. I take off every label and release low-self-esteem to you. I put on the coat you custom designed for me. I am loved, appreciated and accepted. I am a world changer. I overcome obstacles and outlast challenges. I am valued and accepted. Today, I turn the page on labels and low self-esteem. In Jesus name; amen.

CHAPTER 4

TURN THE PAGE AND FORGIVE

There is a woman whose heart was broken when he cheated on you. There is a man who was crushed when you noticed your wife flirting and engaging inappropriately with other men. There is a sister who has been offended for several years. There is a mother who has held on to jealousy of her children's success, wishing it was her own. There is a daughter who was violated by someone she trusted. There is a brother who felt betrayed and left to fend for himself. There is a widow whose heart was shattered into a million pieces when the love of her life was taken too soon. There is a child who lost a parent too early and an adult who watched their parent suffer in their last years. There is a sibling who doesn't understand why they always seemed to be left out. There is a son in law who has been ostracized. There is a daughter in law who was led to feel she was never good enough. There are parents who

blame themselves for the heartache their children

experienced. There is a spouse who serves the communi-

ty as a police officer, fire fighter or military personal and

you thought they were coming home but didn't, their last

day on earth was spent serving our country. There is

someone who had a preacher, teacher, professor,

politician or important leader in your life who complete-

ly let you down. Unless
someone has walked in your
shoes, no one will understand
your pain. When there is hurt
and pain all around, when does

> *"The bleeding in life stops the moment you forgive. Forgiveness leads to healing."*

it stop? The bleeding in life stops the moment you

forgive. Forgiveness leads to healing. Healing brings

restoration to your spirit and soul. Our soul is made up of our mind, our will and our emotions.

It is said that high blood pressure is a silent killer. So is unforgiveness. High blood pressure, causes damage to artery walls and can cause heart disease, stroke and organ damage when untreated. Unforgiveness untreated, leads to a life of bitterness, hardness, incarceration, unhappiness, discontentment, regret and remorse. Unforgiveness damages your inner man. When we are offended, we are taught to let it go, get over it, move on, but are we really indeed letting go and moving on? Most people harbor the unforgiveness inside and it begins to pile up like a stack of dishes. When you leave dishes in the sink, unclean, they begin to stink. If they are left there for days, a bacteria grows on them. Harbored unforgiveness grows bacteria which ultimately causes infection.

Infection can begin to heal when you forgive. Forgiveness brings healing to your soul. Forgiveness does not justify what the other person did. Forgiveness

> *"Forgiveness says you will no longer let it linger as an unwelcome shadow in life."*

says you will no longer let it linger as an unwelcome shadow in life. People ask me all the time; how do I forgive? I gently, reference the R4 methodology. You must release the hurt so God can remove the pain, restore your life and redeem you to the place you were intended to be. As we learned in the life of Joseph, he was sold out, left for dead, lied on, dismissed, forgotten about, falsely accused, imprisoned, abused by those closest to him, by those who were supposed to love him the most.

In the latter half of Joseph's life, Joseph had been promoted to second in command of Egypt. Egypt was a land that contained resources while others were simultaneously going through a famine. The Scriptures teach us that Joseph and his family had not spoken in many years. Neither of them knew where the other was located and what they were doing these days. While Joseph was leading in Egypt, Jacob, Joseph's father sent his ten sons to purchase food and resources from Egypt. Now remember, they had no idea, they would encounter Joseph neither did they expect him to be second in command. It had been thirteen years, since Joseph last saw his brothers, imagine the shock as he saw them approaching. Joseph had moved on. Joseph was no longer in slavery, no longer in prison, but as his brothers approached, the emotions flooded back. Joseph did not speak to them in their native tongue of Hebrew. He spoke in Egyptian. He spoke to them by way of an interpreter. His brothers had no clue it was him. The moment Joseph saw his brothers, although he did not know what they wanted, he had to decide if the pain of the past would resurface and boil or if he would turn the page and forgive.

Joseph's heart was broken as he stood face to face with the very ones who set the calamity of his life in motion. As they stood in front of him, they began to explain they wanted to purchase resources. At that moment, Joseph had the authority to have them executed. If you were confronted with those that hurt you, would you take revenge? Joseph spoke roughly with them and accused them of being spies. He had to decide

at that moment: do I forgive or take revenge? He

honored his brothers' request, sent them back with

food, but kept one brother as collateral because he

wanted to see the youngest brother. He told them to

bring the youngest brother. Joseph had never met him.

His brothers went home and returned with Benjamin.

As they returned together they had dinner, Joseph still

did not disclose who he was nor did the brothers

recognize him. In addition to it being thirteen years

since they had seen each other, Joseph, by this time,

was skillfully trained by the Egyptians so his behavior

mirrored the Egyptian culture not the one into which he

was born. When the brothers left, Joseph purposely put

his drinking cup in Benjamin's bag. He told his soldiers

to follow them and when they get so far to stop them

and find his drinking cup. The soldiers did as they were

told and brought them back to Joseph. Joseph asked

"Why have you done this to me?" "What have I done to

you?" They went back and forth and finally before

Joseph reached his breaking point, he asked everyone to

leave the palace room except his brothers. They had no

idea what to expect. It was at that moment, the games

stopped and Joseph revealed himself to them.

Joseph wept so loud. In the shedding of tears, he

was shedding the pain. He was releasing the bitterness

of rejection and the sting of betrayal. He was turning

the page on the day they sold him into slavery, on the

days he spent in prison, on the days he was wrongly

accused, on the days he was starving and forgotten

about. It was at that moment everything began to make

sense for him. His dreams of his brothers and father

bowing down that offended them so many years ago, it was here and now. Joseph was in a position of authority and his family was need.

He told them, "I am Joseph." He explained God sent him before them to preserve life. He provided a back-story, explaining his story and then dropped the bomb that he forgave them. Yes, he forgave the same people who left him for dead! Joseph knew in the midst of all the pain there was purpose. He faced his purpose and his why was revealed as he revealed himself to them. Up until that point before his brothers came, he always wondered why, but why was revealed in his forgiveness. God pulled back the curtains of his under-standing and the healing began. His purpose, not his pain was the focal point.

When you are hurt, it can sting fiercely; think of a bee sting, but much worse. People deal with different levels of emotional pain. Sometimes they incur physical injury as well. The scripture says in I Corinthians 15:55 (KJV) "O death, where is thy sting? O grave, where is thy victory?" God has noted how death has lost its sting and the grave lost the war. The grave lost the war because this "thing" you have faced and carried, it happened, but it didn't take you out. You see, a bee can only sting you once, once it loses its stinger. It may continue to fly, but it can no longer sting you. God has graced you to overcome. You will not continue to suffer through the emotional sting once you allow God into the healing equation. He removes the sting. He heals the sting. God has graced you to outlast the sting of the offense you are dealing with. The good work God has started in you, God will finish. Invite him to handle your situation and remove the sting.

When you decide to release the situation you not only forgive but you begin to reconcile with what occurred. You can reconcile a situation when you forgive, not hold it as a secret, not bury it, not use it as an excuse, not coddle it, not project your pain on others, not eat it away, not exercise it out, not disguise it, but confront and release it, you are saying "I will live again! This will not take me out." You do not accept what they did nor do you need to reconcile with the person, but you refuse to allow this situation to hold you back. My friend Pastor Rosie Ozuna always said "You know you are free when you can talk about the situation without experiencing the pain of the offense." It hurt past tense but when you are free you are over it.

It's those places that become places we can minister to others from. This is what becomes your testimony.

Joseph's weeping released and reconciled every hurt, discouragement, resentment, and brokenness. The betrayal was so deep, yet it didn't mar his character, integrity, or actions. Another great man from the bible was name David. David at one point felt betrayed by King Saul. To provide context, King Saul was rejected by God. When he realized David was next in line to be king, King Saul despised him. King Saul chased David like a wild animal in effort to eliminate his life. King Saul attempted to make his life miserable. King Saul's son Jonathan showed kindness to David. The Scriptures teach us that when David felt betrayed by King Saul, he didn't harbor it, he did not try to hold ill contempt against King Saul, instead he reconciled with King

Saul's family. David reconciled with Jonathan's son Mephibosheth. He asked if there were any who remained in Saul's house who he could show kindness to, for Jonathan's sake. What he was doing was turning the page on unforgiveness and betrayal. He turned the page on the past and the emotions that could have created obstacles. All the unnecessary opposition David went through because of King Saul, David forgave. David knew Jonathan was a portion of Saul's real heart. King Saul's real heart never would have wanted to hurt David. So this was David's way of making things right.

When you and I reconcile, we annihilate every fear, anxiety, and uncontrolled habit spurred out of the betrayal. Betrayal impacts your ability to trust. Reconciliation re-establishes your ability to trust again. You no longer feel something is owed to you. David could have had Mephibosheth killed, but he didn't. He no longer felt something or someone was owed to him. David even allowed Mephibosheth to sit at the Kings table and eat with David's children. Mephibosheth was blessed because of Jonathan, but used by God to reconcile David and Saul. Reconciliation annihilated the resentment, rejection, and regret. I want to encourage you to release what you have gone through to God. It might be traumatic, it may be a long story and it may have extenuating circumstances or extensive details. You may blame yourself. God wants you to be free.

David found something good from the tragedy and used it as a catalyst to reconcile. Bury the hatched and turn the page. You are too far along, you have too much going for you, there are dreams awaiting you with your name them. Say goodbye to the pain of yesterday and hello to the promises of tomorrow. God knew life would bring betrayals. Judas betrayed Jesus but Jesus forgave him and turned the page. Peter betrayed the Lord, but found repentance and reconciled with God and turned the page.

A man named John told me a story where he felt betrayed by a longtime friend. The two had a phone conversation which turned into a base of lies, misinterpretation and misunderstanding that would impact John for several years. Time passed and John later randomly called to catch up with Kevin another mutual friend. John was excited to share the exciting things God was doing in life and the first thing out of Kevin's mouth was "I forgive you." John said, "This is John Sharp from El Paso." John thought Kevin was confused and thought he's was talking to the wrong person.

Prior, John and Kevin had a great relationship, now the need to forgive. John was confused he had no idea what he did. Kevin began to share what this "brother in the Lord" "shared" with him. John was so hurt by what was said and then equally felt betrayed that Kevin, this person he admired, respected and had an over ten year history with, believed what was spoken. John was crushed, disappointed and angry. He wanted revenge. It was hard to see past the hurt. John wanted to confront the issue, have a three way conference and lay the truth out on the table. He wanted the truth to be spoken and known. He wanted that person to be held accountable for the dissension they were sowing. Finally, one day in prayer the Lord spoke a few things to John. One was to bury the hatchet. That was powerful because in essence the Holy Spirit impressed upon him to turn the page.

John didn't understand why the entire situation occurred. The Lord also showed John that people make up
lies to deflect sin in their own life. God is faithful to
reveal the truth and in time, God did just that. The truth
was revealed. Every top has to stand on its own bottom
and time confirmed John's integrity.

In the book of Proverbs, the bible tells us hope
deferred makes the heart sick. When we lose hope that
is when fear, doubt, anxiety, and depression begins to
creep in. We think hope is lost and we will never
recover. That is a lie. You are a chosen vessel created in
his image. All you have to do is turn the page, there is
forgiveness awaiting you, ready to be unleashed! Your
pain, your lost hope, your hurt may be from something
recent. I know it might hurt even now, but when you
turn the page, you will experience the hope that is in

Christ. Christ's hope is fresh and new. You will experience His divine provision for your dreams because they are not over. You have not run into a brick wall, your breakthrough is on its way.

Do you remember the Nintendo video game Mario Brothers? Mario and Luigi would get this special, supernatural power charge that enabled them to knock out bricks. Sometimes coins would pop up and special power flowers. It's like that in Christ. When you forgive, there is a supernatural, unexplainable, undeniable power that comes over you to move forward and climb over mountains. It's not over. If you recall, every time you have seen a group or a survivor interviewed on a news cast, a common theme they share is they never lost hope. People may not understand the depth from where you have had to fight to get to where you are today, but God knows. Hope has kept you going

and hope will keep you going. Don't lose hope! Let me

explain it like this, hope is the fuel in your car; your

faith is your car. I always say faith stands for "forward,

action in trusting Him." Faith moves us forward, but its

hope is the fuel that keeps my faith moving. Hope says

give it one more day, week, month, year, don't quit.

Hope says brighter days are ahead. When we forgive

and turn the page on unforgiveness, God's grace is

released and gives us rest from the stress, struggle, and

strain that comes from the pain and gives us hope to

accomplish our purpose. Faith and hope release God's

supernatural on our lives. Get ready for purpose and

destiny to collide. Your ability to withstand obstacles

and determination to overcome is supernatural. You

have the victory! You can now stop living life with pain

and start living life with purpose from the pain. This is what helps us turn the page on forgiveness. God spoke in His Word to "Let your light so shine before men that they may see your good works and glorify the Father which is in heaven." It's God's light that exposes our potential, our purpose and reveals the path to live on. His light exposes His goodness in our lives. It changes a hurtful heart to a loving and caring heart. But it's by grace that it is completed.

Forgiving is like rain. Rain is designed to refill, reposition, redirect, and restore. It refills what has been empty. It repositions objects that have been left in the dirt. It redirects the current, and it can restore the land by watering it once more. When we forgive it's like rain in our lives. This rain is going to refill, reposition, redirect, and restore every area of our lives. The bleeding stops and the healing begins.

Refilling our lives causes us to be energized. Think of a phone battery. If the phone is not fully charged, no matter what apps or storage it contains, without the charge the phone is powerless. Once it is charged the phone, apps and storage references are able to function. In our lives we need His refill. Refill of joy, love, peace, anointing, clarity, and so on. It's not that His joy becomes depleted, but ours does and we need a refill.

King David asked the Lord in Scriptures to "fill his cup up." Have you ever been at a restaurant and you ask, "Can you refill my cup?" The server will say "Yes." It's not that you don't have a cup, you want more. Life can withdraw from the cup God has filled up. That's why we need a daily refill. We refill by reading his word and spending time communing with God. Sing, pray, meditate on His Word. If we don't refill we can become lethargic and begin to make decisions that are not a part of our destiny. God focuses on our potential. That is why we must allow Him to refill us; the refilling causes repositioning in our lives. Listen to a message, read a devotional, turn on the Christian radio station refilling is important and you should make it a priority. When you come to the house of God on Sunday or Wednesday or whatever day you go, it's a time to receive and be filled up. Just like a phone needs to recharge, so do our spirits. God wants to refill every area of your life. He wants to refill you spiritually, physically, relationally, career-wise, eco-nomically, mentally, and emotionally. You don't have to wait for a church service to have a moment with

God. Your moment can happen right now. Your refill can begin right now. You have been called to live a victorious life. Who do you need to forgive?

Next the rain will reposition us to the place of more than enough. The rain can cause us to reposition. It's in the repositioning we move toward our destination. Repositioning is what is needed for us to live a victorious and fruitful life. After you forgive, you are able to let go. You stop worrying about

> "When we allow the rain to reposition us, we don't end up out of place, but in the place God originally called us."

certain things. You begin to see life in a different perspective. When we allow the rain to reposition us, we don't end up out of place, but in the place God originally called us. This is the place where God has called us to be, physically, emotionally, financially, and relationally. You feel healthy again. It's like when you visit a chiropractor and receive an adjustment. You are repositioned to walk, bend and move well. Your alignment is on point and you are ready to function at an optimum level.

In your repositioning you have to plan, prepare, and plant. The plan is always directed toward the vision. After you have forgiven, start to trust again, love again. Tell yourself better days are ahead. Decide you will forgive and not regret. Strategies will change, but the vision will remain the same; forgiving others so you can reposition is a constant. Don't associate change with compromise, two different concepts. You can change something without compromising. The plan causes us to prepare. Paul wrote to Timothy to stir up the gift inside. He was saying work and prepare for what your gift is for. When we prepare for what God

has for us, we are ready to plant when the time comes.

When someone cuts you off on the freeway, have you

prepared your heart to thank God they didn't hit you or

are you planting seeds of anger?

The Bible tells us about a farmer that went out

to plant seeds. Some seeds fell on hard ground; others

fell into the thorns, while others fell on good ground.

The hard ground was the area that had no rain and died

from the heat. Then there were thorns that are the cares

of life. There was no faith added to that seed. In other

words you wanted to forgive, but never acted upon it.

Then there is the seed that fell on good ground. Good

ground is productive. Good ground yields a harvest.

Good ground makes you happy and gets you excited to

feel things are going to work out in your favor. Good ground moves you past the offense and onto victory.

Next is redirection, rain will redirect you. I remember the first remote control car my boys requested as a gift. As new owners, they had to learn to steer the remotes in the direction they desired. I had to show them how to redirect the car so that it would drive effectively. The redirection of the remote handle maneuvered the car to the direction of their desire. So it is in our lives. Redirection is God's way of gaining our full attention. God handles the remote control. As we forgive, we stop looking for excuses of why the pain was caused and focus on living life. We begin to redirect our thoughts, feelings, and actions.

Let's look at the Bible. Abraham journeyed to the land of Canaan. When he arrived, there was famine in the land, so he went to Egypt. Egypt was not his place of destiny so God redirected him. Elijah was another man in the Bible who God redirected. Elijah hid in a cave at one point in his life. He felt alone and abandoned. God whispered to him, redirecting his life that indeed he was not alone. Elijah went on to pursue greatness prior to his departure to heaven.

Lastly is restore. God is in the business of restoration. He tells us He will restore the years the locust has eaten, the cankerworm, the caterpillar, and the palmerworm. That sounds a little science oriented but it has significant meaning. In the original Hebrew translation according to the Strong's concordance, the word locust means sudden disappearance and insignificance. God is saying He will restore what the enemy has made insignificant in your life as well as anything that the enemy has quickly tried to take from you.

Maybe it was innocence, maybe it was your life, and

maybe it was a promotion or a relationship. The devil is

a liar. He does not have the last say. You have made it

through. You survived. Now it is time to thrive. God is

able to restore to you what has been lost. What the

enemy has tried to make insignificant in your life, God

will heal. What you have been through does not define

you nor does it devalue you. The enemy aimed to make

you feel less than but you are more than and you will

win in life. You are just as special today as you were

the day you were born. If heaven had Instagram the day

you were born, you would have been all over it. The

day you were born you would have been trending on

Facebook and Twitter with a grand announcement

because the call on your life and the purpose you were

created for is incredible. You are just as special and significant today as the day you were born. God is proud of you and who you will become. It doesn't matter how old you are. Your future is great. The years you feel you have wasted; God will restore time unto you. You do not have to live one more day feeling inadequate and in a deficit. God is a restorer. Restoration happens after the rain. When land has been dry for a long period of time, the rain begins to restore it. It causes the seeds and the original grass to grow back. I have seen ground that has not had any rain, but the moment the rain begins to come, the grass starts to grow. The grass begins to grow back greener than it was before. The reason is the seeds are still alive. You have seeds alive inside of you planted with your purpose.

In Joel 2:25, the next word God uses to illustrate restoration is the word cankerworm. It's the Hebrew Word, "Yehlek." According to the Strong concordance it means a young locust and early stage of development. God was saying He will restore the early years the enemy robbed from your life. If you were shortchanged, given the short-end the stick, your restoration is on its way. If you had any type of loss during your early development God will restore those years as if you did not go through it.

The Scripture uses the word caterpillar, the Strong's concordance breaks it down to mean to devour and eat away. What has devoured your life will be restored. The almighty has authored a plan of restoration for you and your life. It's not over; turn the page on unforgiveness. God is not through with your life story.

The final chapter has not been written. All you need to do is turn the page.

Don't allow time to consume you. Let time work for you. It takes five years for a bamboo stick to grow. Year one through four, you cannot see much progress from the bamboo stump, but the moment it hits year five, it sprouts up to ten feet. What could take you ten years, God can accelerate in a year. It's like the bamboo stick, while it is under water you cannot see its progress and growth. Do not allow what seems invisible to hinder you. When you forgive, you have turned the page on unforgiveness. You have allowed the rain to set in and position you for acceleration.

Unforgiveness is a time stealing, life devouring, hope killer. It robs you of time God has given you on earth. It limits how far you go, it whispers don't trust and don't let what they did go. It keeps you from God's best opportunities. I have a colleague who shared with me a low point in life where he allowed the voice of pain to speak so loud he operated from a place of hurt most days and devalued the sermons he put together weekly. He directed his staff to not record him for one year. He believed no one wanted to hear him speak. What a joke, his congregations was full every Sunday in a good size auditorium, yet the enemy convinced him, he had nothing to say week after week. One day he realized he had to turn the page and forgive those who hurt him. He had to take off the label others put on him and the one's he put on himself. The opinion of a few not liking a sermon was not the majority. It's a real struggle for preachers. The enemy plays on your mind weekly. Not just preachers, but I know educators who wonder week after week if they are really making an

impact. Professionals in healthcare sometimes wonder

if it's all worth it. The enemy wants to wear you down.

Run your race. This preacher is one of the best preach-

ers I know. Do not silence your voice. Do not throw in

the towel. Turn the page on unforgiveness.

A PRAYER

Father, I come before you in the name of Jesus. I forgive those who have done me wrong. I ask you to forgive me for the times I have been hurtful as well. I let go of all the animosity, hatred and bitterness associated with the unforgiveness in my heart. I face it, trace it and replace it with your love and healing. I turn the page on unforgiveness in Jesus name; amen.

CHAPTER 5

TURN THE PAGE ON LACK

Lack is a deficit. Lack comes in a variety of forms and packages. People can lack love, confidence and sufficient time to complete what God has put on their heart. Lack is anything you are short in or short of. My father always said, "The enemy only fights what he fears." Many times you will find the enemy tries to place lack in your life where it ties to your purpose. This is because it is his objective to impair your efforts. The thermostat of life is not validated upon what you have. Instead it is by what you do with what you have. Mass and matter do not limit God. That is why if God has given you a dream, He is more than able to see it come to pass.

> *"If God has given you a dream, He is more than able to see it come to pass."*

In the Bible there were four leprous men that sat at the gate of the Kingdom. Leprous people were not allowed to live in the city. To provide context, the country was at war and food was scarce. The four leprous men were desperate and said to one another, "Why stay here and die? If we surrender ourselves to the enemy, they will either enslave us or kill us but it would be better than starvation." In their unique rational, they went to the enemy's camp in hopes to be enslaved and fed. You may think it was a crazy move, why would anyone want to surrender themselves to the enemy? However, for these guys, they felt it was a small step of faith in an effort to live. Little did they know that God had already prepared an ambush on the enemy so when they arrived, the camp was empty. Not only was the camp empty, it was also full of food, resources and weapons available for the leprous men and their entire kingdom that was in lack back home. A little back-story, the reason the enemy evacuated was because God made a sound as though there were thousands of soldiers ready to invade. Those four leprous men ate, and then sent word back to the king. It was confirmed and just as the prophet had prophesied the day before, food and resources were again available. Sometimes in life, we may feel like there is no hope and there is no way of getting out. God has a way already prepared for you, He simply needs you to move out and take a step of faith. God is ready for you to turn the page on your lack.

Anna loved her husband. They had been married almost eight years and she was feeling her marriage was in trouble. They had two children and the couple was well established in their careers. She frequently

complained about how her husband was often being

pulled away by work. She felt she was always the one

to compromise her career. In reality, she was blessed

with a position that offered greater flexibility than her

spouse. In reality, yes, her husband had a demanding

career but most successful individuals are pulled by

their career demands. It's what you do with it that

counts. Think about it for a moment. If your husband is

a coach, he needs to be up at the field-house to open it

up and work out with the kids, sometimes leaving the

house at 6am not coming home till 7pm. If your

husband is a doctor, there are weeks, after hour calls are

all his. If you husband is in business or administration

of any kind, some work days can end at 7pm then by

the time he gets home, it's after 8pm. If your husband is

a pastor, every weekend you're at church, every day of the week he is ministering to one family or another, he is pulled away for church business and if your husband is a politician, after long hours at the office, his speaking engagements take up the evening. If your husband is a builder, guess what? The home owners are able to meet on weekends and after work hours which means he's not coming home till 8pm. The enemy always tries to make it seem like the grass is greener on the other side. Sometimes perceived lack also comes down to a lack of understanding. James 1: 5 (NLT) says, "If you lack wisdom, ask of the Lord." What Anna needed to understand is that all marriages have seasons and all careers have their extra hours.

I shared a story with Anna about my sister-in-law and brother-in-law. My brother- in- law Victor is an extraordinary athlete and gave back to others prior to

working in education administration by coaching. My

brother-in-law is a runner. Not just any runner, but he

was a state champion in his day. He was generous

enough to pay forward to students across Texas how

they too could be state champions. As you know, to

become a champion long hours are involved. Coaching

requires long hours. I remember my brother-in-law

would coach at cross country meets across the state as

his students would compete. My sister-in-law Melissa

could have easily stayed at home with her two small

children at the time but she decided to make it a family

fun event. She would pack up their two young

daughters; and meet everyone at cross country meets.

Diaper bag, snacks, drinks, activities, blankets, stroller

and all other supplies in tow, she would make it out. I

know lots of woman today who would say "No thanks see you when you get home." Although, my brother-in-law would only see them for a few minutes, knowing they were there on the sidelines cheering the team on made a world of difference. This strengthened their marriage and family bond when it could have equally torn it apart had she stayed home weekend after weekend, long day after long day. Today they have three children, two grandchildren and continue to teach the principles of turning the page and making the most of every situation. It's an admirable trait and family value.

So many times, people believe the grass is greener on the other-side. My wife Veronica tells me that they use to visit her dad up at the fire-station when she was little. Today, that is fun memory looking back.

TURN THE PAGE TODAY   Mark Brown

When it occurred, it was her mother maximizing their
time with their daddy while he served the community
on shift work ensuring the city was safe as a first
responder. Our family friends, The Gamboa's, Javier
works long hours at the hospital. His family goes up to
visit and quickly say hello or drop by a lunch or dinner.
Those small jesters are a family making the most of
their season in life. Lack can be eliminated, it requires
creativity and initiative but you can do it. Lack comes
down to perspective. Lack can be turned around just as
the aforementioned families turned the lack of time
around. Anna realized that day dreaming of her
husband changing professions wasn't going to change
anything. He is less than ten years away from

retirement and to throw it away because of perception,

> "She didn't allow the voice of lack to speak louder than the voice of increase. She did not allow the voice of doubt to speak louder than the voice of faith"

turning the page on lack requires we adjust our perspective in life. There was a woman in the Bible that brought a debt concern to the attention of the prophet in their city. The first thing he asked her after she shared her story was "What do you have in your house?" Although, she was coming with what she felt was nothing, God was getting ready to show her what she could do with the little she had. The little she had in her house God was ready to multiply. The prophet instructed her to "Go and borrow all the vessels you can. Then go into your house shut the doors and windows and then begin to pour." The woman did

exactly what the prophet said and she began to pour the

small amount of oil into every pot. She didn't allow the

voice of lack to speak louder than the voice of increase.

She did not allow the voice of doubt to speak louder

than the voice of faith. She filled

all the vessels she had with the

"Do not base your future off of your fears"

oil that supernaturally did not

run out. She had enough to pay her debts. Do not base

your future off of your fears. When you think you are

out of resources God will provide. He just needs you to

use what you have. When you use what you have, you

turn the page on lack.

Lack of vision can create a shortage of hope. I encourage you to re-evaluate your perspective and then turn the page. Dreams do not have deadlines. When you obey what God has spoken for you to step out on, you will experience the reward of obedience.

> *Dreams do not have deadlines. When you obey what God has spoken for you to step out on, you will experience the reward of obedience.*

Where you are going is greater than where you have been. The pressure of pleasing man and giving up is not a greater than the reward of obedience and following through. Don't allow lack to be an excuse in your life. Noah could have used the lack of rain as a viable reason to not build the ark. However, what

> *"The pressure of pleasing man and giving up is not a greater than the reward of obedience and following through."*

God has you building can change the course of the future and the world. Say this with me: I am turning the page on lack today. I release all my frustration, my time line, my way and take hold of your way, wisdom, and understanding.

God is the creator of the Universe. He created the atmosphere and the entire environment. What He calls you to do; He also gives you the ability to accomplish. Before former President Abraham Lincoln became the 16th President of United States of America, he went through some challenging times. In fact, he went from being bankrupt to brokenhearted. He lost in most of his political runs yet, he never lost sight of pursuing his passion. Many believe he was one of the greatest presidents to have lived. People believe he changed the world by not allowing the opposition to change him. What has God Almighty placed in your

heart that you need to pursue? Pursue all that God has

given you. A great preacher, FF Bosworth first said

during the depression era, "You have to doubt your

doubts and believe your beliefs!" It starts with turning

the page on lack.

Timing is everything and you may feel you lack

time to accomplish your dream. With God it is never

too late. There is a neighbor I know who was working

on his law degree. He dreamed of moving his family to

a ritzy neighborhood because that was his heart's

desire. He felt it was never going happen. Law school

was long, and then the potential to be hired on with a

reputable firm earning enough salary to cover school

loans, two children, a wife, plus a new life-style was

slim. However, God honored his pursuit. After he

passed the bar, a large firm hired him and shortly after they moved out of the subdivision. It's not a lofty dream, but it was his dream. Our timing is not the Lord's. Don't allow your age to determine the timing. Turn the page on lack of time. Mary was fifteen years old when God used her to become the mother of Jesus. Abraham was ninety-nine years old. Moses was eighty. Josiah became king at seven years old. Do not limit God by your age.

      I know of a pastor who felt led of the Lord to start a church at the age of fifty. He was a retired Captain in the military, a successful business man and

> *"Age is never a precursor of when to go, God's voice is."*

starting a church was not on his agenda. He recently passed at seventy-six years of age and in his short time pastoring, he accomplished more than what other pastors did in forty years of ministry. In twenty-six years, God did the supernatural. He turned the page on lack of time. He could have declined starting a church at the age of fifty. He could have retired and toured the world. He chose to finish his race. Age is never a precursor of when to go, God's voice is. President Ronald Reagan was sixty nine years old when he became the President of the United States of America. He didn't allow his age to deter him from running for the highest office in the land. God will do more with less time if you turn the page on lack of time. Your future depends on you.

In the Scripture, it teaches us to not cast our pearls before swine. God was telling us not to waste time with situations or non-essentials in life. What God has for you and me is greater than the swine or non-essentials of life. You have been called by God to build

> *"Comparing limits us and incarcerates our God given talents."*

and nothing is to distract you.

We should stop comparing and

continue to build what God has

placed in our hearts. Comparing

limits us and incarcerates our God given talents. It says

I will only do a little more than the other person. It

becomes a copy instead of being an original. You are an

original. There is nothing like the original. What God

has created for you is original. Turn the page on lack of

confidence and comparison.

You are not a victim you have been given the

victory. Lack is not God's desire.

Lack is eliminated in and through

our giving as well. The Scripture

teaches us that giving reduces

> *"You are not a victim you have been given the victory."*

lack. If your marriage is suffering and lacking love, start by saying or doing something nice for your spouse. If you lack financially, evaluate where you are and where want to go. Create a gap analysis thereafter, sowing towards filling in the blanks. That's right sow a seed of faith towards where you want to be financially. There was a young couple that just completed two years of marriage. They were saving up to get another car and didn't have much money. They decided to sow a seed of faith and give an amount in honor of what they believed God for, as they searched for their vehicle. The following week, when they visited a car lot, the manager said, "Let me show you something I don't have on the floor yet. I can afford to give it to you at what I brought it in at because I have already hit my numbers for the month. I remember being young and needing something dependable so let me give you my best." That type of story is unheard of. It's remarkable, but we serve a remarkable God. This young coupled sowed into their financial future by faith. Recently, my wife needed another vehicle. She knew exactly what she was looking for down to the price, make, model, mileage, warranty, color of exterior and interior, you name it, she had it worked out. She called a dealership out of Houston and unbeknownst to her the sales manager answered. She reminded him of his daughter and as she began to wheel and deal, this manager gave her exactly what she was looking for. This was favor and harvest for the many seeds she had sown in the past. When you give monetarily, you are sowing. God will supply your needs. Today, I want to encourage you to turn the page on lack. You might need to call someone, give something, or simply let something go, but turn the page of lack. Stop allowing lack to tell you, you will never love like you should. You will never lead like you should; you will never parent like you should. No, tell lack, I am a godly man, I am a godly woman. I am leading with God's authority, I am healed, and I am prosperous. I am going over not under. I walk with grace and mercy surrounding me. I am a child of the Most High God. My father owns the cattle on a thousand hills. This year, will be my best year yet!

A PRAYER

Heavenly Father, you are the creator of the Universe. There is no lack in you. I submit to you every piece of my heart and every area of lack in my life. I declare my needs are being met and I will come out ahead and not behind. I declare lack is over today! I declare I will live in the overflow. I turn the page on lack. In Jesus name; amen.

CHAPTER 6

TURN THE PAGE ON SETTLING

Sometimes the fight is too fierce and the battle is too long so we decide to settle. Sometimes there have been too many battles and you have decided to quit fighting. I challenge you today to not settle. What do you need to pick back up? What excuses have you allowed to get in the way?

There was a man who was a corporate trainer for a large organization. It was very challenging for the new employees to master concepts at the onset because it was so much to learn so quickly. The trainer's effectiveness was measured on the success rate of the trainees. The trainees had thirty days to prove they had it or didn't. Each new employee was a student for thirty days. It was an intense boot-camp. This one trainer was named Mario. Mario was a seasoned trainer, not for this company but in life. He was a retired Marine. He was motivated. He refused to allow anyone to neither settle and be the status-quo nor give up and quit, much less fail.   The first day of class, trainers were required to go over rules, requirements and expectations. After the basic rollout and before beginning lecture for day one, he would tell his class "There is only thing you do not have permission to do." Everyone was always very serious waiting with expectation for this major, important hard stop rule and he would continue "You do not have permission to fail. I will not allow you to fail. I will be with you every step of the way. I believe in you. I know the next thirty days will be difficult but you will make it through. You will not fail!"

That brief pep talk set his class apart. His success rate was always 100%. He had the same curriculum, the same amount of time, the same random selection of adult learners but when it came down to evaluations that was the one differentiating factor. By telling his class they did not have permission to fail, he was essentially saying he would help them fight through every excuse that would prevent them from graduating in thirty days. Our outcome is reflective of our attitude along the journey.

Right now in life, it is not a time to settle. God has more for you than where you are. Sometimes we settle because those around us don't see us where we see ourselves, so we continue to stay in the cubicle not reaching for more. I urge you to not hold your life standard by how others perceive you but by the dream God has placed in your heart.

Joseph from the Scriptures was never trained to handle the opposition he encountered. There was no preparation and he could have easily accepted and settled for the life in prison or as a slave. However, the anointing on his life is what brought him to his success. Did you know you are anointed? You may be anointed to be a police officer and you are required to have a clear understanding between the letter of the law and the spirit of the law. You may be anointed to do business. My brother Jacob, when we were little and would go to bible camp, he would bring candy and sell them when the concession stand was closed. He would come home with more money than what my parents sent us with every time. He knew how to multiply the resources he had and maximize the situation. Today he is a successful business man. That is his anointing that has been apparent since we were very young. You have been anointed. Maybe it's to bring healing to patients through medicine or administration. We all have gifts.

God is counting on us to not settle but maximize our

gifts. One thing I have realized in speaking with thou-

sands of people is that many settle when they encounter

a group like Joseph's brothers or maybe it's a King Saul

or a Miriam. God has victory in your future. Do not

allow settling to be part of your life story.

I recall this woman Lucy. Lucy was pregnant

and lost her child while in the womb. It was devastating

to her, her husband and their family. No one knew

really what to tell Lucy that would console her, her

heart was broken and she needed time to grieve. Her

husband was likewise devastated but men and woman

process differently. The enemy would plant thoughts in

her mind that it was her fault or that her body failed

which resulted in the miscarriage. On good days, she

wouldn't think about it. On days when she saw infant or

baby clothes at a store or anything that would trigger,

memories would begin to surface and intrusive thoughts

would play in her mind. I remember Lucy coming up to

ask for prayer. I prayed healing over Lucy, her body,

her mind, every part of her being. I prayed God would

restore and we ended the prayer believing God for his

goodness over their family's life. Years and years past

and I lost contact with Lucy and her family. I remember

encouraging them and letting her know that what she

was experiencing; the pain, the hurt and the lack of

understanding, it wasn't a place to build camp and

settle. Grieving is a process and in time, it would be

time to move forward and turn the page as God healed

every aching piece of their heart. We prayed if it was

God's will that they would conceive again. If not, that

God would have his perfect will in their life. These

situations are so delicate, every situation is different but

it is important to keep the grieving process moving

forward towards healing. God is faithful to bring

healing in His time and His way. The best thing we can

do for situations we do not understand is gently pray.

Pray for the Father's will and for the Father's hand to

touch and minister to the family in their respective

situation as only He knows how.

Years later, at least eight years down the road, I

had a woman approach me who I didn't recognize with

a child. She said, "It's me, Lucy, this is my son Michael

we prayed about all those years ago." My heart was so

thankful because this family didn't settle in their faith.

Even if their son Michael was never born when a family

goes through a traumatic experience it can rock their

faith. They didn't settle in their walk with God and dismiss God as a side gig but they continued believing God for great things. They continued serving God. Even when it didn't seem they would have another child, they continued and today by his grace they have a son. Everyone has a different story, but I encourage you today that when you have an event that rocks your world, do not settle in the despair of the situation but push your way through to the other side. Joy does come in the morning. Sometimes in life, you can hit a season when you feel like all hope is lost. You feel like "it's over" whatever good was going on has come to a close. Well, I want to remind you today, that when one door shuts, another one opens.

There was a young woman named Lisa. Lisa got married at an early age, got pregnant and end up having the marriage annulled. Not the happy ending she went

in hoping for. She tried to find Mr. Right and that didn't

quite work out as she planned. She started going back

to church and dedicated her life back to Christ. She

focused on getting her life back on track and decided

she would no longer settle for the average Joe. She

raised her daughter as her only child and several years

down the road, Lisa met Harry. Harry and Lisa married

and today have three children together, Harry raised

Lisa's first child as his own and the couple is now near

their forty year anniversary mark. You see Lisa decided

to turn the page on settling. She could have taken a

multitude of different routes but chose not to. Settling is

a choice. She could have settled to be single and

struggle or push to be single and successful. When

people want to quit on you, when places seem out of

reach, and you want to give up on yourself; God is still there. Throughout the Bible, we come across people that have encountered great failures and yet at the same time turned them around into great triumphs and comebacks.

I knew a builder named Robert. Robert didn't start as a builder. He started as a sub-contractor who specialized in framing. He didn't have much. He told me that other framers urged him leave the area and travel with them to find new work. That would have been settling for the status-quo in his field. He decided to wait out the dip in the housing market. As time passed he would get work here and there. One day, his break came when a realtor encouraged him to develop some land, encouraged him to not only frame houses on the land but to be the general contractor. The timing was right in the area after the housing market bubble.

He moved on that advice and today he stands as a

multimillionaire. It was not an overnight process. It

didn't come without tests and trials both in the industry,

with his family and his marriage. He refused to settle.

He endured the hardship associated with risk, and today

he has reaped the rewards.

You have been given the ability to succeed in

every area of your life. It is up to you, to not settle and

push your way though. When God instructed the spies

to spy out the land of Jericho, they focused on the

impossibility of conquering the land. They felt like

grasshoppers as the Scripture mentioned and would

have settled in their discouragement and inferiority if

their leader had not pushed them to their promise. God

is your leader. He wants you on the other side of

settling. Only you know what you have been putting off for years. Get to it!

In the Bible, there was a man name Samson. He was the strongest man that had ever lived. In fact, the Bible tells us there had never been nor will be a man that was as strong as Samson. As amazing as Samson was, he also had weakness, as we all do. Only this weakness lasted until it destroyed him. Settling can be a weakness and it can destroy you, if you do not take

> *"What you do not confront you cannot overcome."*

hold of it. We must confront and conquer in order to win. What you do not confront you cannot over-come. Samson wanted to do right, but was always entertaining this weakness and settling. This weakness cut his future short. You have to be ready and willing to change, not ready and wanting to change. Willing takes you to action, wanting is the root that holds settling as a habit in your life.

Your past is not an indicator of the future, God's Word is. There was a woman in the bible that was caught in the act of adultery. She was taken from the scene and thrown at Jesus' feet. At that

> "Your past is not an indicator of the future, God's Word is."

moment the leaders were trying to catch Jesus in a lie. Jesus stooped down and wrote in the sand and then stood up. He said those who have no sin cast the first stone. Not one leader was left to accuse and throw a stone, they all walked away. It does not matter what your past holds. What your past holds does not determine your future. It is unknown what Jesus wrote, but I believe in the sand, her future was being outlined as He showed his grace and mercy in the situation. Today, your future has been outlined and greater days are ahead for you! Don't give up! Don't bow out.

God never makes a mistake. He didn't make a mistake when He created you. He didn't make a mistake when He sent His only Son to die on

> *"You are not a mistake. You were born for greatness."*

the cross for our sins. You are not a mistake. You were born for greatness. Don't allow the past to be an indicator of the future. Think of Thomas Edison, if he had quit, how long would it have been before electricity would have been discovered? What about Penicillin? Alexander Fleming discovered penicillin and it marked a true turning point in human history. Don't stop, don't back up, or refuse to give in. God has all of heaven backing you up. It seems like nothing is working right, or it has become too difficult, know God masters in the impossible. When we do our part, God does His part. In other words, you are an over comer. You have God's resilience residing on the inside. You may need to regroup, refocus, but don't quit. Turn the page on settling.

In life it is easy to settle because the pressure you face is significant. It's easier to give in when the pressure is on. You might need to step aside take a deep breath, and exhale, but don't settle. I know it gets hard or tough at times, but the God we serve is more than able to help us along the way. Be willing to go the extra mile. Our faith is the pivoting point of our attitude. Staying with it requires commitment.

> *"Commitment is the breeding ground for harvest."*

You must have no quit in your game!

Commitment is the breeding ground for harvest.

When we are committed to something, we invest into it.

When we are committed to God's vision for our lives,

we live and invest the same. It becomes part of our life.

It's staying committed even when it's hard. Commit-

ment breaks the habit of settling.

When God created you He created you with

purpose and destiny. He created you to outlive the

failure, frustration, hatred, and lies of the enemy. If you

were placed in a room with someone that was one

hundred years old they probably would tell you to run

your race, not looking to the right or the left. Run fast.

Run hard. They would tell you to count the cost, and

pay the price. They would tell you life is short. Then

they would say your latter will be greater than your

former, don't settle, don't quit, keep moving forward.

They would let you know that what others say is not as important as what God has you focusing on.

A PRAYER

Heavenly Father, I give you all the areas of my life I have settled in. Forgive me for not pursuing purpose and not pushing through. I release to you the prior disappointments in life that have discouraged me and influenced me to settle. I declare from this day forward I will not accept the status quo. I will not settle for mediocrity. I was born to be more than a conqueror and I declare I will walk in victory. In Jesus name; amen.

CHAPTER 7
TURN THE PAGE ON QUITTING AND INCONSISTENCY

Pastor Jones shared with me it was a calm and clear day as he sat in his office and reached a significantly low moment. He was facing horrific opposition and was under mountains of stress. He had become so discouraged that as he looked at the walls around his office, showcasing his degrees and various accomplishments, he sunk his head between his chest and wondered what is this all worth? The enemy of our soul was working overtime in efforts to convince him to devalue what he had worked for and the work his ministry had accomplished to date. The preacher decided to get up from his desk and take a break. He turned on his phone, accessed an app and began to watch a Christian TV program. When he turned it on, immediately the preacher on the show, pointed into the camera and said, "God is telling you pastor to stay in that city." Right then the Holy Spirit began to encourage this pastor. Only God knew he was questioning if he was in the right city. The preacher on the program began to prophesy that God would turn this all around for his good. The Man of God was inspired, never quit and went on to fulfill his purpose.

Have you ever felt this way? God has sent me today to tell you, all things will work together for your good. You will make it to the other-side. You see this preacher had to acquire a stance that this journey is worth the fight. You need to decide in your spirit that your fight is worth it too. Your journey may be different than the preachers, but we are all human and need to depend on God's supernatural strength to make it through. The Bible tells us, to whom much is given, much is required. God will complete the work He has started in you.

There were two brothers in the Bible named Esau and Jacob. Esau was an outdoorsman, while his brother Jacob was a farmer. Both of these men were great, but only one reached his destiny. One day, Esau came from the wilderness. He had been hunting all day but did not catch anything. Esau visited his brother and saw he prepared soup. Esau asked Jacob if he could have some soup. Jacob told him Esau "Sell me your birthright for a cup of soup." Esau said according to Genesis 25:32 (NLT) "Look, I'm dying of starvation!" "What good is my birthright to me now?" Wow! What a statement of defeat. Esau allowed his emotions to devalue his own birthright. It had only been one day Esau was without food.

Some of us might get hungry in areas of our life, but it doesn't mean we sacrifice the permanent upon the altar of immediate. Don't throw in the towel just because it's not going the way you want or because you are starving. You are not alone. Jesus said "I go before you and prepare a place." God is always preparing us for great things. We have to refuse to quit. If you stop, you will not see how it finishes.

A few years back when the economy went south, many commercial buildings where left unfinished on one of our major freeways. You would drive by them for a few years and would only see a metal frame. I often imagined what building design the frame would take on as it reached a finished out state. One day, I noticed work resumed after years of delay on the project. Once it was complete, it was beautiful. Every time, I see these buildings I am reminded of the work one can begin while another finishes. Someone picked up where someone left off. That happens in life sometimes. We are forced to pick up where someone else left off. Others are forced to pick up where we quit.

In life, we may question ourselves, "What good is this degree, marriage, and life?" You may be ready to throw in the towel. The enemy will use opposition as a place of defeat. Throw in the towel on quitting. The enemy likes to play on our emotions to get us to feel like giving up. Esau sold out because he felt he was going to die. He was far from death, but his emotions took over his mainframe unit and he gave up. Don't associate the feelings of yesterday with the promise of today. The promise is still on. Feelings will deceive you. Don't go on what you feel, but on what God has instructed you. When your mind is telling you to quit, don't!

If you are starving in an area, whether it is acceptance, love, respect, touch, or other areas, don't give up what belongs to you. You have not come this far to sell out for a bowl of soup. Jesus never gave up. He went all the way to the cross. Daniel, Shadrach, Meshach and Abednego never gave up. Shadrach, Meshach, and Abednego stayed faithful even though they were thrown into the firry furnace. Daniel was thrown into a hungry den of lions. Both survived without a burn, scratch, and were promoted.

If you are single and tired of being alone; do not settle. God has the right

"Do not confuse disagreement with incompatibility."

person for you. If you are married and experiencing

marital woes, do not confuse disagreement with incompatibility.

Do you remember the story in the Bible where Jesus told His disciples to go to the other side yet a storm arose? This storm was so intense, the disciples' thought they were going to die but Jesus came out walking on the water to them and calmed the winds and the waves. Here we see God gave the disciples the word to go to the other side. Whatever you are facing today, your word is to go to the other side. The word did not fail the disciples and it will not fail you.

The pressure that seems insurmountable and is bearing down like a beast, I declare God is pushing it back even now as you continue to read. I declare the supernatural power of God Almighty is working things out for your good. I declare favor is coming your way and no weapon formed against you will prosper. The Scripture teaches us when the enemy comes in like a flood; the Spirit of the Lord will lift up a standard.

I know people who instead of quitting decide to cover up. Covering up leads to inconsistency but at the root of the issue is someone wearing a mask. I invite you to allow the Great Physician to heal the areas you want to cover up. When you feel overwhelmed, I want you to lean on this scripture: "I can do all things through Christ which strengthens me." Philippians 4:13 (NLT)

A PRAYER

Heavenly Father, forgive me for quitting, giving up, throwing in the towel and not moving forward. I release to you all of my procrastination, inconsistencies and lack of follow through. You have destined me for greatness. You are the source of my supply and I tap into your well of strength and endurance. I am who you called me to be. I am strong in you. I declare I will accomplish all you have set out for me and when I stand before you, you can say "well done." I turn the page on quitting and inconsistency. In Jesus name; amen.

CHAPTER 8
HOW TO BEGIN AGAIN, LIVE AGAIN, AND DREAM AGAIN

Your "again" starts when you turn the page. We have established to turn the page we must release so God can remove, restore and redeem. As we let go of the rejection, devastation, fear, setback, labels, low self-esteem unforgiveness, lack, settling, quitting and inconsistency God has so much more in store for you.

> *"God is waiting for you to step into position and overcome life's opposition."*

Living in faith every day is possible. Walking in victory is possible. Your success story has already been written. God is waiting for you to step into position and overcome life's opposition.

As a young child I enjoyed working on model airplanes. I specifically recall one project that was so overwhelming my frustration hit a peak and I threw the plane on the floor. The model shattered into more pieces than it was meant to be built with. My father walked over and picked up the pieces in a calm manner.

He placed everything back on the table. He said "Mark,

I know you can do it, you have done it before." Later

that week, I completed the project. Many of you

reading this book have had your model airplanes of life

shattered. Just as my dad picked up the pieces, today

your heavenly father is picking up your dreams and

telling you, you can begin again, live again and dream

again.

- When Ruth was rejected and God gave her the
  opportunity to begin again, live again and dream
  again.

- When Moses fled after he killed an Egyptian, he
  felt his dreams were shattered. God stepped in,
  called him and commissioned him to live again.

- When Peter walked on the water he began to sink as he saw the wind and the waves. He cried out to Jesus and immediately, Jesus picked him up and they both walked hand in hand back to the boat. Today, Jesus wants to pick you up from where you are sinking so you can begin again. He is telling you, He is here and ready to walk hand in hand with you.

In the Old Testament, there were men called Apothecaries. They compare to modern Pharmacologists and they were instructed by the Lord when and where to cut a spice or herb. They would use these to prepare the holy, anointed incense. There were some sweet and some sour; a total of nine. As they were combined, they became sweet incense. God does a similar work in our lives. He takes the amalgamation of our life experiences, the good, the bad and the ugly. He

mixes them together to work for our good. God will use

everything you have been through so you can

successfully begin again, live again and dream again.

There was a man in the bible named Lazarus.

He was Jesus friend. Lazarus had become ill and by the

time Jesus arrived to pray for him, Lazarus was dead.

He had been dead for four days. Family and friends

moved him to a tomb. When Jesus arrived He said

paraphrased, "Everything is going to be okay." How is

everything going to be okay when someone is dead?

Jesus told them to roll away the stone. Martha was

hesitant because of the odor that would come from the

tomb of a dead man. Some of us have dead areas in our

life, the pain, grief, hurt, disappointments and anger has

a stench blocking opportunities to live well. But God

wants to resurrect the buried dreams in your life. Jesus resurrected Lazarus that day. Jesus said "Lazarus come forth!" Today I speak to your dream "Come forth!" When Lazarus came out, he was wrapped like a mummy, Jesus then said "Loose him and let him go!" I declare right now that as you turn the page you too will be loosed and let go! You will be able to live again!

Turn The Page Today!

A PRAYER

Heavenly Father, I thank you for loving me. I declare today I have turned the page. I declare freedom over my life to begin again, live again and dream again. I declare I am whole, complete and not looking back. My best days are ahead of me and I will be the person you have called me to be. I will walk in victory and not defeat.   In Jesus name; amen.

30732157R00113